OSPREY
PUBLISHING

# The Sarmatians
# 600 BC – AD 450

R Brzezinski & M Mielczarek • Illustrated by G Embleton

Series editor Martin Windrow

First published in Great Britain in 2002 by Osprey Publishing
Elms Court, Chapel Way, Botley, Oxford OX2 9LP, United Kingdom
Email: **info@ospreypublishing.com**

ISBN 1 84176 485 X

Editor: Martin Windrow
Design: Alan Hamp
Index by Alan Rutter
Map by John Richards

Originated by The Electronic Page Company, Cwmbran, UK
Printed in China through World Print Ltd.

FOR A CATALOGUE OF ALL BOOKS PUBLISHED BY
OSPREY MILITARY AND AVIATION PLEASE CONTACT:

**The Marketing Manager, Osprey Direct UK**
**PO Box 140, Wellingborough,**
**Northants, NN8 2FA, United Kingdom**
Email: **info@ospreydirect.co.uk**

**The Marketing Manager, Osprey Direct USA**
**c/o MBI Publishing**
**729 Prospect Avenue, Osceola, WI 54020, USA**
Email: **info@ospreydirectusa.com**

**www.ospreypublishing.com**

## Acknowledgements

The authors would like to thank Nick Sekunda for his unfailing assistance throughout this project; John Rohde for his insightful comments on the text; and Martin Windrow and Anita Hitchings of Osprey for their saintly patience while this book was taking shape. All images are from the authors' collections unless otherwise specifically credited.

## Author's Note

Over a millenium separates the Sauromatae of the 7th century BC from the Alans of the 5th century AD. During this period they were a key element in the nomad hordes which swept in from Asia and combined with Germanic tribes to destroy the Roman empire in the West. Yet the Sarmatians left no written history of their own, and what exists is one-sided, being mainly of Greek and Roman origin. Pictorial material showing Sarmatian warriors is also mostly non-Sarmatian, and requires careful interpretation. The most reliable information comes from excavated artefacts, but these are often from aristocratic burials, which are not necessarily representative of the warrior class as a whole; in many cases the archaeological evidence contradicts the written and pictorial sources. Clearly, reconstructing the appearance of Sarmatian warriors is a complicated exercise, and has never previously been attempted on the scale of this book.

## Artist's Note

Readers may care to note that the original paintings from which the colour plates in this book were prepared are available for private sale. All reproduction copyright whatsoever is retained by the Publishers. All enquiries should be addressed to:

Gerry Embleton
Time Machine SA, La Chaine 15,
CH 2515 Prêles, Switzerland

The Publishers regret that they can enter into no correspondence upon this matter.

# THE SARMATIANS 600 BC – AD 450

TOP **Obverse of a bronze coin of the Bosporan king Rhescuporis II (AD 69–93), showing him trampling on a defeated barbarian, perhaps a Sarmatian, while another long-haired tribesman kneels to the left. A trophy of arms including long trousers and helmet with cheek-pieces stands at the right.** ABOVE **The goddess Nike on the reverse suggests minting to commemorate a military victory, while the letters 'MH' indicate a value of 48 units or sesterces. (Muzeum Archeologiczne i Etnograficzne, Lodz, Poland)**

## WHO WERE THE SARMATIANS?

THE SARMATIANS were not a unified people, but rather a number of groups of nomad peoples of similar stock, who wandered generally westwards over the Eurasian steppe – the vast corridor of grasslands, hundreds of miles wide and some 5,000 miles long, extending from China to the Hungarian Plain. They spoke an Iranian language similar to that of the Scythians, and closely related to Persian.

The Sarmatians emerged in the 7th century BC in a region of the steppe to the east of the Don River and south of the Ural Mountains. For centuries they lived in relatively peaceful co-existence with their western neighbours, the Scythians[1]. Then, in the 3rd century BC or slightly earlier, they spilled over the Don to attack the Scythians on the Pontic steppes to the north of the Black Sea (Pontus Euxinus), and 'turned the greater part of the country into a desert' (Diodorus 2.43). The surviving Scythians fled westwards and sought refuge in the Crimea and Bessarabia, leaving their pasturelands to the incomers. The Sarmatians were to dominate these territories over the next five centuries.

The best known of the Sarmatian peoples were the Sauromatae, Aorsi, Siraces, Iazyges and Roxolani. The Alans were essentially of the same Iranian stock as the Sarmatians, but are often considered a distinct people. These groupings were tribal confederations rather than individual ethnic tribes; indeed, Ammianus Marcellinus (31.2.13–17) and medieval Arab sources state specifically that the Alans were a coalition of different peoples.

Most Sarmatians were nomads whose grazing herds provided much of the food and clothing they required. They wintered on the southern fringes of the Russian steppe, close to the Black and Caspian Seas and Russia's great rivers, heading north for pasture in the spring. Accompanying them were their covered wagons which doubled as homes – Ammianus Marcellinus notes (31.2.18): 'In them husbands sleep with their wives – in them their children are born and brought up'.

The early Sarmatians are now generally regarded as the reality behind the myth of the Amazons. According to Herodotus (4.116), women of the Sauromatae hunted, shot bows and threw javelins from horseback, and went to war dressed in the same clothing as men. This has been confirmed by archaeology: early Sarmatian female graves often contain bronze arrowheads, and occasionally swords, daggers and spearheads; while skeletons of girls aged 13 and 14 have bowed legs – evidence that, like boys, they were often in the saddle before they could walk. The status of women was so unusual that some writers

1 See MAA 137, *The Scythians 700–300BC*, E.V.Cernenko & M.V.Gorelik (Osprey, 1983)

Only two of the 400 scenes on Trajan's Column depict Sarmatian cavalry (top right). The riders and horses are covered head-to-toe in scale armour, even the horses' hooves being armoured – clearly an exaggeration, but equally clearly the Roman perception of the Roxolani was that their horses were protected by some sort of bard. Lances were originally fixed to the Column but have long since vanished. Note also the 'draco' standard carried (top left) by a Dacian warrior. (After C.Cichorius, *Das Relief des Traiansäule*, Berlin 1906)

(Pseudo-Scylax, 70) believed that women ruled Sarmatian society.

During the 1st century AD the Sarmatians and Alans truly began to enter recorded history when they conducted a series of spectacular raids on their civilised neighbours. Pouring into Asia Minor, they spread devastation among the Parthians, Medians and Armenians. At the same time other Sarmatian groups ravaged Rome's Danubian provinces of Pannonia and Moesia, before pushing their way along the lower Danube and into the Hungarian Plain to establish a more permanent presence. Some took up military service with the Romans, but for centuries Sarmatians remained unpredictable neighbours, starting wars at the slightest provocation. The pressure was so great that the Romans eventually allowed many to settle within the empire. It was largely as a result of the Sarmatian wars that the Roman army began to abandon its reliance on the legionary infantry and develop an effective cavalry arm – for which the lance-armed Sarmatian cavalry were to provide one important model.

During this time the Sarmatians maintained close contacts with the Greek centres on the northern Black Sea coast, in particular the kingdom of the Cimmerian Bosporus[2]. At its peak the Bosporan Kingdom covered the eastern part of the Crimean Peninsula, the western part of the Taman Peninsula (then an archipelago), and the mouth of the Don. In the mid-1st century AD a dynasty of Sarmatian origin came to power in the Bosporan Kingdom and both state and army were 'Sarmatised' – to such a degree that Bosporan heavy cavalry cannot be distinguished from their Sarmatian counterparts. Indeed, Bosporan art is one of the historian's best sources for Sarmatian weaponry.

The emergence of the Goths was to destroy the Sarmatians' relationship with the Bosporans. The southward migration of the Goths from Scandinavia via modern Poland to the River Dnieper was under way by about AD 200; by about AD 250 the Goths had taken Olbia and moved east to the Crimea, replacing the Sarmatians and Alans as the dominant power of the region.

A century or so later, the arrival of the Huns from Central Asia was no less traumatic. As waves of Huns and Goths set about tearing the Roman empire apart, the Alans could do little but follow obediently in their wake. The currents drew them as far afield as Gaul, Spain and North Africa. Sarmatian and Alan contingents, ever smaller and less significant, also fought with the Romans. By the mid-5th century the Sarmatians were no longer in control of their own destiny, and by the 6th century little trace of them remained in western Europe. They had not disappeared, but rather had been woven seamlessly into the colourful tapestry that was to emerge as Medieval Europe.

---

2 This northern Bosporus near the Crimea is now usually spelt without an 'h', to distinguish it from the Bosphorus near modern Istanbul, at the mouth of the Black Sea.

# CHRONOLOGY

Sarmatian history is divided by archaeologists into the following periods:

7th–4th centuries BC – Sauromatian
4th–2nd centuries BC – Early Sarmatian
2nd C BC–2nd C AD – Middle Sarmatian
2nd–4th centuries AD – Late Sarmatian

**c.507 BC** Sauromatians help Scythians repel an invasion of the Pontic steppe by King Darius I of Persia.

**310/09 BC** Aripharnes, king of the Siraces, commands Sarmatians at battle of Thates River in support of Bosporan pretender Eumelos.

**179 BC** Gatalos, king of Sarmatians in Europe, mentioned in peace treaty between nations of Asia Minor.

**107 BC** Roxolani support Scythians against Crimean city of Chersonesos, but are defeated by Diophantes, general of Mithridates VI Eupator of Pontus.

**16 BC** First Sarmatian incursions over lower Danube beaten off by Romans.

**AD 34–35** Sarmatian mercenaries fight under Pharasmanes of Iberia during Parthian civil war.

**AD 49** Siraces and Aorsi supply troops to rival factions in Bosporan succession war; Siraces' town of Uspe sacked by Roman faction.

**AD 50** Iazyges supply cavalry to Vannius, Roman client-king of the Germanic Quadi, in his war against rival tribes.

**AD 69** Some 9,000 Roxolani raiders are defeated in Moesia during spring thaw by Legio III Gallica.

**c.AD 73** Alans raid Parthia, devastate Media and defeat Armenian king Tiridates.

**AD 92** Iazyges, Quadi and Marcomanni invade Pannonia, defeating Legio XXI Rapax.

**AD 101/02** Roxolani support Dacians during Trajan's first Dacian campaign.

**AD 105/06** Trajan's second Dacian campaign: Dacian kingdom destroyed, Roman province of Dacia created.

**AD 135** Alans raid Media and Armenia, but are repulsed from Cappadocia by the Roman governor Arrian.

**AD 167–80** Marcomanian wars: Iazyges support Germanic tribes against Rome.

**AD 173/74** Iazyges invade Pannonia, but are defeated at 'battle on the frozen Danube' by Marcus Aurelius.

**AD 175** Iazyges make peace with Rome and supply 8,000 warrior-hostages, of which 5,500 are sent to serve in Britannia.

**AD 236–38** After campaigns against Iazyges, Maximinus Thrax is titled 'Sarmaticus Maximus'.

**AD 282** Iazyges defeated in Pannonia by emperor Carus.

**AD 297** Sarmatian auxiliaries fight in Galerius' war in Persia.

**c.AD 334** Slaves of the Danubian Sarmatians revolt and rename themselves 'Limigantes'.

**AD 358–59** After revolting against Rome the 'Free Sarmatians' submit, but the Limigantes are slaughtered en masse by Constantius.

**AD 375** Huns smash Gothic power north of the Black Sea: the 'migration period' of European history begins.

**AD 378** Alan cavalry play key role in the crushing Gothic defeat of the Romans at Adrianople.

**AD 409** Invasion of Spain by Vandals, assisted by Alans and Suevi.

**AD 429** Alans accompany Vandals into North Africa and set up kingdom (to AD 533).

**AD 451** Alans under King Sangiban fight at battle of Catalaunian Fields in Gaul.

**AD 453** Alans fight for Attila the Hun at battle of Nedao River in Pannonia.

**AD 453** Death of Attila: Hunnic 'empire' collapses.

Another scene from Trajan's Column, showing Sarmatian horsemen fleeing from the Roman onslaught. One armoured rider (top right) shoots a 'Parthian shot' back at his pursuers. The horses' eye-guards are copied from Roman equestrian sports equipment: nothing similar has been found in Sarmatian graves. (After C.Cichorius, *Das Relief des Traiansäule*, Berlin 1906)

# THE SARMATIAN PEOPLES

By 1000 BC the Eurasian steppe, from the Black Sea in the west to the Altai Mountains in the east, was occupied by nomad peoples of similar culture and Iranian language. An archaeologically distinct series of Sarmatian groups began to appear south of the Urals in around the 7th century BC. To their east in Central Asia emerged the Dahae, Massagetae and Sakas. These 'Asiatic Scythians' were genetically related to the Sarmatians and had a strong influence on their development.

Classical authors divided 'Sarmatia' into European and Asian parts, the boundary being the Don (Tanais) River – the ancient frontier between Europe and Asia. How far 'Sarmatia' extended eastwards into Asia is still the subject of debate. Until recently large parts of western Siberia were regarded by Western scholars as culturally Sarmatian, but as 'Central Asian' by Russian archaeologists. Either way, 'Asiatic Scythian' and Sarmatian cultures were very similar.

The meaning of the term Sarmatian has been variously explained by modern historians. Perhaps the most entertaining derivation is from the Greek word *sauros*, suggesting 'lizard people' – supposedly inspired by their dragon standards and reptile-like scale armour. This is, of course, nonsense. Most historians now agree that 'Sauromatae' is a variant spelling of 'Sarmatae', first seen in texts of the 2nd century BC (Polybius 25.2); indeed, Pliny the Elder (4.80) states that one was the Greek spelling, the other the Latin: 'Sarmatae, Graecis Sauromatae' (though to complicate matters further, Greek authors often use the Latin spelling.) But we do have a better idea of what the Sarmatians called themselves: Greek authors of the 4th century BC (Pseudo-Scylax and Eudoxus of Cnidus) mention neighbours of the Scythians living near the Don called 'Syrmatae'. Meanwhile the Avesta, the holy book of ancient Persia written down in c.500 BC in an early dialect of Iranian, mentions a region 'to the west' called 'Sairima'.

In the following paragraphs we list the main Sarmatian groups and attempt to give an outline of their histories. However, the wanderings of these peoples over the centuries are complex and defy compartmentalisation. Most nomad peoples contained a fusion of different tribes rather than persons of a single ethnic stock. By their nature the Sarmatian peoples were highly mobile; they mingled freely with neighbouring tribes, formed alliances, coalesced and then broke up again.

Clay model of a Scythian wagon-dwelling, 4th–3rd century BC, found in the Crimea at Kerch (ancient Panticapaeum). Strabo mentions the seasonal migration of the Sarmatians in such wagon-homes, in search of pasture. Spoked wheels have replaced the solid wheels seen on earlier wagons. The wagon body was probably made of wicker, while the framework at the rear would normally have supported a thick tilt, usually of felt (Strabo 7.3.17), made from the coarsest grades of wool and animal hair, or of tree-bark (Amm. 22.8.42). Four- or six-wheeled wagons were pulled by two or three yoke of hornless oxen (Hippocrates, *Peri Aeron*, 18). According to Strabo (7.3.18), the horns of Sarmatian oxen were shorn off, being sensitive to the cold of the steppe. (Archaeological Museum, Odessa, Ukraine)

## The Sauromatae

The Sauromatae (Greek 'Sauromatai') are the earliest of the Sarmatian peoples recorded in written history. In the 5th century BC Herodotus (4.21) wrote that they lived to the east of the Don River, in the treeless lands that extended for 15 days' journey north of Lake Maeotis (the Sea of Azov). Herodotus' Sauromatae seem to match an archaeological culture that thrived in the 7th–4th centuries BC between the Don and Volga rivers, reaching to western Kazakhstan, and stretching north from the Caspian Sea to the southern Urals.

Most of what is known about the Sauromatae is semi-mythical. Herodotus (4.110–116) states that they were the children of a union between Scythians and Amazons (whose home several

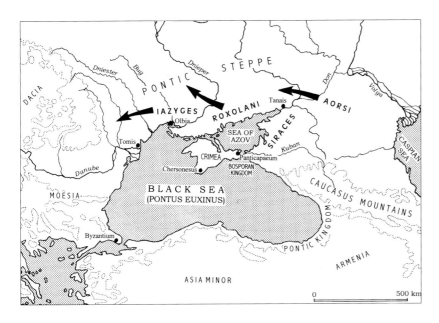

ancient authors place north of the Caucasus). Their language was a corrupt form of Scythian, 'since their Amazon mothers had never learnt it properly'.

The recorded history of the Sauromatae begins and ends with a single event: in c.507 BC (the date is uncertain) they fought as allies of the Scythians in a war to prevent the Persian King Darius I from invading the Pontic steppe. The Sauromatae contingent even marched as far west as the Danube in an attempt to hinder the

**The main Sarmatian tribes as described by Strabo (c.68 BC–c.AD 26). The Iazyges and Roxolani lived on the northern Black Sea (or Pontic) steppes before migrating towards the Danube. The Siraces remained in the Kuban; while the Aorsi, after several centuries spent between the Volga and the Sea of Azov, were pushed westwards by the Alans arriving from the east. Panticapaeum was the capital of the Bosporan Kingdom, which included many Greek centres on the Taman and Crimean peninsulas.**

Persian army's operations.

In the archaeological sense 'Sauromatian' is a convenient label for the earliest period of Sarmatian history (7th–4th centuries BC). The Sauromatae were a key sub-set of the Sarmatian peoples, and they influenced other Sarmatian groups as these gradually moved westwards and entered the historical record.

**The Siraces and the Aorsi**

In the late 5th century BC the Siraces (Greek 'Sirakoi', Latin Siraces or Siraci) migrated from Kazakhstan to the Black Sea region, and by the late 4th century occupied lands between the Caucasus Mountains and the Don, gradually becoming masters of the Kuban region. They were the first Sarmatian group to have contacts with the Greek settlements on the Black Sea coast. In 310/309 BC King Aripharnes of the Siraces intervened in a succession war in the Bosporan Kingdom, only to see his troops defeated in a pitched battle on the Thates, a tributary of the Kuban River.

The Siraces were a relatively small nation, but Strabo (11.5.8) says that their king Abeacus was able to raise 20,000 horsemen during the reign of the Bosporan ruler Pharnakes (63–47 BC). The Siraces aristocracy preserved a semi-nomadic lifestyle, but much of the population had become settled. They were the most Hellenised of the Sarmatians, and maintained close contacts with the Bosporans.

On the open plains to the north and east of the Siraces lived the Aorsi (Greek 'Aorsoi'), one of the more powerful Sarmatian confederacies, who had likewise migrated from further east. Strabo (11.5.8) distinguished two branches of the Aorsi, one living closer to the Black Sea and able to field an army of 200,000 horsemen, and the still more powerful 'Upper Aorsi' who 'ruled over most of the Caspian coast'. Current thinking suggests that Aorsi lands extended east as far as the Aral Sea.

Some scholars identify the Aorsi with a people known in Chinese chronicles as the Yen-ts'ai (or An-ts'ai). The Chronicle of the Earlier Han dynasty (Han-shu), written down in about AD 90, states that 'their trained bowmen number 100,000'; and that they lived 2,000 *li* (1,200km) north-west of K'ang-chü (Sogdiana), a state that dominated the fertile Oxus-Jaxartes region (Transoxania) south-east of the Aral Sea. Later Chinese sources comment that the dress and customs of the Yen-ts'ai were similar to those of K'ang-chü (Hulsewe, p.129).

During the Bosporan War of AD 49 the Aorsi supported the pro-Roman faction, while the Siraces aided their opponents. During this war the Romans besieged the Siraces' fortified centre of Uspe, but its wicker-and-mud walls were so weak that according to Tacitus (*Ann.* 12.16–17): 'Had night not stopped the conflict, the siege would have been begun and finished within one day'. Uspe quickly fell by storm and its population were slaughtered, scaring the Siraces into submitting to Rome. The war of AD 49 greatly weakened the Siraces, and little more is heard of them until another Bosporan conflict in AD 193, after which all trace of them vanishes.

In the meantime the Aorsi seem to have been conquered or absorbed by a powerful new Sarmatian confederation, the Alans, who were emerging from the Central Asian steppes. Some of the Aorsi were pushed further west, north of the Crimea where, for a time, they maintained a semi-independent existence. Ptolemy refers to the 'Alanorsi', suggesting that a fusion of some form had occurred, though the two groups were probably closely related. Somewhat later, the Chinese chronicles state that the Yen-ts'ai (Aorsi?) had now changed their name to 'Alan-liao'.

### Iazyges and Roxolani

Of the many postulated meanings of the name Roxolani (Greek 'Rhoxolanoi'), the most convincing derives from Iranian *raokhshna* – 'light' or 'white'; in the language of the nomads 'white' often means western – giving 'Western Alans'. The meaning of Iazyges (Greek & Latin) is uncertain, but the term usually appears as Iazyges Sarmatae, suggesting that they were part of the original Sarmatian horde.

The Roxolani and Iazyges were among the vanguard of the Sarmatians who established themselves west of the Don. While the Iazyges hugged the coast near the Crimea, the Roxolani roamed further north across what is today southern Ukraine. In 107 BC the Roxolani, led by Tasius, intervened in a conflict in the Crimea, during which they faced the army of King Mithridates VI Eupator of Pontus. According to Strabo (7.3.17), the mixed Roxolanian-Scythian force '50,000 strong, could not hold out against the 6,000 men arrayed with Mithradates' general Diophantes, and most of them were destroyed'. After this defeat many Sarmatians went over to Mithridates and campaigned in the Bosporan Kingdom; they also fought in his wars against the Romans (Appian, *Mithr.* 15, 19, 69; Justin 38.3, cf. 38.7).

In 16 BC the Sarmatians (probably Iazyges) had their first recorded brush with Rome, when the Proconsul of Macedonia drove them back across the Danube. For the next three centuries Sarmatian incursions became a regular occurrence on Rome's eastern frontier.

Nomad horse-archer hunting wild boar, depicted on an enamelled gold belt fitting. He has a pony-tail hairstyle, and a scabbard-slide is used to sling the sword. The object comes from the 'Siberian Collection' of Peter the Great, assembled in 1716 and now in the Hermitage, St Petersburg. The collection is said to have originated in Siberia, but many objects probably came from looted *kurgans* in Central Asia and the Volga and Black Sea regions.

The poet Ovid saw several such incursions during the years AD 8–17 when he was in exile at the Black Sea port of Tomi (modern Constantsa, Romania); he described the Sarmatian horsemen and their wagons crossing over the frozen Danube during the winter.

The Iazyges headed north-west from the lower Danube, and by the middle of the 1st century AD had arrived on the Hungarian Plain between the Danube and Tisza rivers. In AD 50 they came to the aid of Vannius, the Roman-appointed king of the Suevi, who had been driven from his kingdom by Germanic neighbours. The Iazyges provided Vannius with his only cavalry, but when he shut himself up in a fortress the Iazyges, 'who could not endure a siege, dispersed themselves thoughout the surrounding country', and Vannius was quickly defeated (Tacitus, *Ann.* 12.29–31).

Lancer of the 3rd century AD, armed in Sarmatian manner, from the marble stele of Tryphon found in the ruins of the Bosporan centre of Tanais on the Don, which was then dominated by the Alans (Ammianus' 'Tanaitae'). The clean-shaven, long-haired rider wears a rounded cap or helmet, without cheekpieces or neckguard. His scale corselet is secured by a broad belt, and worn over a long-sleeved under-garment and trousers. The rider's legs seem to curve under the belly of his relatively small horse. He holds his long lance with both hands. (After Rostovtsev)

By this time the Roxolani were living to the north of the lower Danube (Pliny the Elder, *Hist. Nat.* 4.80–1). From AD 62 they made repeated raids on Roman Moesia, the largest of them in the winter of AD 69 (with the participation of 9,000 men) and in AD 85–86. During one of these raids they destroyed a Roman legion (Suetonius, *Dom.* 6.1). During Rome's Dacian wars of AD 85–88 and AD 101–05, the Roxolani sided with the Dacians.

For the greater part of this period the Iazyges were friendly with Rome, and even served as allies in the hope of obtaining lands within the boundaries of the empire. But the creation of the province of Dacia by Trajan in AD 106 pushed a wedge between the Iazyges and the Roxolani, antagonising both peoples. Calm was restored when Hadrian allowed them to maintain contact through Dacia, began paying subsidies to the Roxolani, and made their king Rasparagnus a Roman citizen.

Major disturbances resumed during the Marcomanian Wars (AD 167–80), when the Iazyges combined with several Germanic peoples to attack Pannonia and Dacia. The Iazyges lost a substantial force after a battle against the Romans on the frozen Danube in AD 173/74. Two years later they made peace; Marcus Aurelius took the title 'Sarmaticus', and the Iazygian king Zanticus agreed to hand over 8,000 horsemen as hostages. The greater number of these troops ended up in the province of Britannia (Dio Cass. 72). For a time there were plans to incorporate Iazyges lands within the empire as the new province of Sarmatia.

Peace reigned for nearly half a century, until the eruption of the Goths into the Ukraine set off another chain-reaction of disturbances. After a campaign against the Iazyges in AD 236–38 the emperor Maximinus I (a Thracian, with a Sarmatian mother) assumed the title 'Sarmaticus Maximus'. The Iazyges invaded Dacia in 248–50 and Pannonia in 254, but were defeated in Pannonia in 282 by the emperor Carus (AD 282–83). Battles against the Iazyges continued throughout the reign of Diocletian (AD 284–305).

During the 3rd and 4th centuries AD the Romans allowed several mass resettlements of Sarmatian peoples within the boundaries of the empire, mainly as a foil against the Goths and a source of manpower for the army. The *Notitia Dignitatum* lists 18 centres of Sarmatian settlement across Gaul and Italy. Traces of military settlements survive in place-names like Sermais and Sermiers, near Rheims, which itself hosted a Sarmatian base. Many Sarmatian nobles obtained Roman citizenship, and some rose to positions of power – most famously, Victor, Master of Horse under the emperor Jovian (c.363 AD).

The Hungarian Plain was now regarded as the ancestral homeland of the Danubian Sarmatians, though fresh Sarmato-Alan blood continued to arrive from the east. The Roman authors now speak only of the Sarmatians or 'Free Sarmatians' and their former slaves, the Limigantes. After the Huns arrived in the Danube region and on the Hungarian Plain in the 370s AD it is no longer possible to trace the Roxolani and Iazyges as distinct peoples.

## The Alans

In the mid-1st century AD, soon after Rome's first contacts with the Iazyges and Roxolani, a new wave of immigrants from Central Asia pushed into lands north of the Caspian Sea and Caucasus Mountains. The Alans (Greek 'Alanoi', Latin Alani) had coalesced from a disparate group of tribes, not all of Sarmatian origin. Ammianus (31.2.12) says that the Alans[3] were formerly called Massagetae, while Dio Cassius (69.15) is even more direct: 'they are Massagetae'.

The once powerful Massagetae had gone into decline in the 2nd century BC, and alongside them in the Alan ranks were a goulash of 'Asiatic Scythians', including descendants of several Saka peoples of the Oxus-Jaxartes region and other Central Asians. Ammianus (31.2.13) states that the Alans borrowed their name from a mountain range, but today the term is thought to derive from the ethnic designation 'Aryan' and its cognate 'Iran' (Encyclopaedia Iranica, I, 1985, p.803). Not all historians accept this etymology, however. At first, Roman authors confused the Alani with the Albani, a powerful people of the Caucasus. One of Nero's grandiose schemes shortly before his abrupt death in AD 68 was a campaign to conquer the 'Albani', who some scholars consider as a mistake for the Alans.

The first major Alan incursion came in c.AD 73 and, if Josephus (*Bell. Jud.* 7.7.4) is correct, it entered Parthia from the east side of the Caspian Sea, progressing via Hyrcania and Media into Armenia, where the Alans defeated the local king Tiridates in battle. This route suggests that many Alans were still living to the north-east of the Caspian. In AD 135 the Alans made another huge raid into Asia Minor, this time via the Caucasus, and again ravaged Media and Armenia; they were eventually turned back by the Roman governor of Cappadocia, Arrian, whose short essay 'Battle order against the Alans' explains the tactics employed to defeat them. (Arrian's much larger work, the *Alanica*, is sadly lost.)

By the early 2nd century AD the Alans were well established on the lower Volga and Kuban, in the former lands of the Siraces and the Aorsi (whom they had pushed west or absorbed). Alan power seems to have extended further west, encompassing much of the Sarmatian world, which for the first time had a relatively homogenous culture.

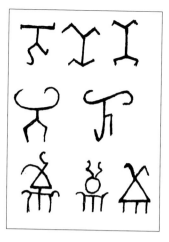

*Tamga* marks from the northern Black Sea area. They appear in this region from the 1st century AD as horsebrands, on weapons, and as graffiti on monuments. Some of them were used as the personal marks of high status individuals and developed into an early form of heraldry. They may originally, like runes, have had a semi-magical purpose. (After V.S Drachuk, *Sistemy znakov Severnogo Prichernomor'ya*, Kiev 1975)

OPPOSITE **A bearded Sarmatian warrior armed with a spear. He wears a close-fitting jacket and trousers, both with decorated seams, and a cloak fastened at the neck by a circular brooch. Detail from a metal *rython* (drinking horn) found in the Kuban, 1st century BC or later. (Hermitage, St Petersburg; after Rostovtseff)**

3 The spelling 'Halani' used by Ammianus is a transcription error from the Greek.

**Tamga** design on an openwork
Sarmatian bronze belt buckle,
2nd century AD. (Archaeological
Museum, Odessa)

The arrival of the Goths in c.AD 215–50 broke Alan dominance of the Pontic steppe. The Alans retreated, mainly to the Don, though enough of them remained to teach the Goths horsemanship, and to give them the taste for Sarmatian fashions and 'animal style' ornaments.

By this time the influence of Huns on the Alans was already becoming apparent. The Alans had maintained contacts with them since the 2nd century AD. Ammianus (31.2.21) wrote that the Alans were 'somewhat like the Huns, but in their manner of life and their habits they are less savage'. Jordanes (126–7) contrasted them with the Huns, noting that the Alans 'were their equals in battle, but unlike them in civilisation, manners and appearance'. These peaceful relations were sundered when the Huns suddenly attacked the 'Tanaitae' or Don Alans, killing many of them and entering a pact with the survivors (Amm. 31.3.1). With these Alans in their ranks the Huns defeated the Goths in AD 375 before pushing on to the Hungarian Plain, where they set up a more permanent presence.

Other Alan groups and neighbouring Sarmatians escaped west with the Goths, and it was one such group who helped the Goths defeat the Romans at Adrianople in AD 378, where the Emperor Valens was killed. As the Roman empire began to fall apart, the Alans also broke up into several groups, each of which wended its complicated path across Europe. Some fought in Roman service, others joined the Huns, the Ostrogoths or the Visigoths. On the last day of AD 406 one of the Alan groups, together with the Vandals and Suevi, crossed the frozen Rhine into Gaul, which they devastated. Three years later they reached Spain and gave it the same treatment. Though the Vandals massacred many of their Alan allies in c.AD 416, when he invaded North Africa the Vandal king continued to style himself *Rex Vandalorum et Alanorum.*

When Attila died in AD 453 the Hunnic 'state' died with him. The Hunnic army, always a hotch-potch of conquered nations, dissolved into parts which spread out in different directions, sending Europe into the Dark Ages. Though pockets of Alan settlement remained, notably in northern France and Catalonia ('Goth-Alania'), where there are dozens of placenames like Allainville and Allaincourt, the Alans had effectively disappeared from history by the 6th century AD. Only one Alan group survived as a coherent nation. When the Huns had first made their devastating appearance on the Pontic steppe this group had quietly slipped off southwards into the sheltered valleys of the Caucasus. Here they flourished into the Middle Ages; and here their descendants, the Ossetians, live on to this day – still teaching their children of their Alan legacy.

**Other Sarmatian peoples**

Many lesser Sarmatian peoples are mentioned by Classical geographers. Most are recorded just once and little more than their name is given; for the following there is slightly more information. The

Saii were one of the dominant tribes of the south-western Ukraine soon after the eviction of the Scythians. According to the Protegenes inscription of the early 2nd century BC, their king Saitapharnes received tribute from the once mighty trading centre of Olbia. Saii probably means 'multicoloured', which in nomad usage refers to horse colours (Harmatta, 1970, p.11). The Basileans or Royal Sarmatians are mentioned by Strabo and Ptolemy, living between Bessarabia and the lower Danube; they were probably the successors to the Royal Scythians. The Iaxamatae or Ixibitai are mentioned by several ancient authors, living close to the Sea of Azov. Pomponius Mela (c.AD 43) writes that the Iaxamatae women 'perform just like the men in war'. They are often assumed to be predecessors of or identical to the Iazyges, but this has recently been questioned.

## APPEARANCE & COSTUME

The Roman poet Ovid, exiled (AD 8–18) to the Black Sea port of Tomis, left a striking picture of the Iazyges crossing the frozen Danube in winter (*Tristia*, 3.10):
'They keep the cold at bay with skins and breeches,/ Of the whole body just the face is left, with icicles the hair will often tinkle/ And beards are white with frost below their lips.'

Despite such rare glimpses of the Sarmatians, they remain a shadowy people; far fewer images survive of them in art than of their Scythian cousins. Like the Scythians, Sarmatians were of a white or Caucasoid appearance, and before the arrival of the Huns it is thought that few had Asiatic or Turco-Mongol features. Yet Sarmatian physiognomy was sufficiently alien to the Romans that Tacitus (*Germania* 46), writing in c.AD 98, called them 'repulsive in appearance'. This should not be taken literally: barbarians rarely matched Mediterranean ideals of beauty.

Sarmatian noblemen often reached 1.70–1.80m (5ft 7ins–5ft 10ins) as measured from the skeletons, and they had sturdy bones – evidence of the nomad meat-and-milk diet. Like the Scythians, they wore long hair and beards. The Sarmatian rulers of the Bosporan Kingdom are usually portrayed on coins with long hair, the younger men clean-shaven or with moustaches, and mature men with dense beards (though coin portraits of this time do not always reflect reality). According to the 2nd-century AD Greek author Lucian (*Toxaris* 51), the Alans wore their hair much shorter than the Scythians. Images of the

**Bosporan or Sarmatian lancer, on a 19th-century copy of a lost 2nd-century AD tomb painting from ancient Panticapaeum – modern Kerch, in the Crimea. His helmet appears to be of banded construction, akin to Parthian examples, which appear narrower when seen from the front. Beneath his large cloak he wears an armour corselet, which could be either scale or mail, and is split at the side revealing an unarmoured thigh. The lance is wielded two-handed rather than couched. (After Rostovtsev)**

'Asiatic Scythians' from which some of the Alans descended often show short hair or pony-tails, and faces clean-shaven except for moustaches. Ammianus (31.2.21) was even complimentary about the Alans: 'Nearly all the Alani are men of great stature and beauty; their hair is somewhat yellow, their eyes are frighteningly fierce.' The yellowish hair is puzzling, but Ammianus sometimes borrowed ethnographic material from earlier authors without checking it. He may be contrasting a mousy brown with the darker hair of his Roman readership – or simply confusing the Alans with the Goths, though some intermarriage is known to have occurred.

Another Alan fashion, cranial deformation, is better attested. An elongated head shape was obtained by bandaging the head in infancy. The custom had appeared on a limited scale among the early Sarmatians, but came into its own between the 2nd and 4th centuries AD (probably under Hun influence) among the Alans on the lower Volga, where up to 70 per cent of excavated skulls are deformed. Deformed skulls are also found in 4th–5th century Alan graves in western Europe.

Pliny (*Hist. Nat.* 22.2) mentions that both Sarmatian men and women 'inscribed their bodies' with tattoos. Sextus Empiricus (3.202) adds that Sarmatian children were tattooed in infancy. Stylised animals were the most likely designs, similar to those on the ice-preserved human skin of 'Asiatic Scythians' from the Pazyryk tombs in the Altai Mountains[4]. Since Sarmatian tattooing receives little attention from other Classical authors it may have been practiced by only some of the Sarmatian peoples.

The costume of the Sarmatians was similar to that of better documented nomad neighbours to the west and east. Many garments were worn little altered until the Middle Ages, and later by the Caucasus Alans and their descendants the Ossetians. The Iranian names for the garments are often preserved in Ossetic and Persian, and have sometimes passed into Slavic languages.

Bare-headed Sarmatian warriors on a belt-fitting from an unknown findsite, perhaps 4th or 3rd century BC. Both riders are spear-armed, and one (right) has a *gorytos* combined bowcase and quiver slung from a waistbelt on his left side. Both wear quilted kaftans, the 'collars' of which appear to be torques. (Historical Museum, Moscow, after M.I.Rostovtsev, *Antichnaya dekorativnaya zhivopis na yuge Rossii,* St Petersburg, 1913)

The main garment was a short kaftan known as a *kurta* which opened at the front and was wrapped across the chest from right to left. Typically this was of deerskin leather, sometimes of woollen cloth. Trousers or *saravara* could be of loose-fitting cloth in Parthian style or more closely fitted and of leather. Undergarments were often woven from hemp: 'anybody who has never seen a piece of cloth made from hemp would suppose it to be of linen'(Herodotus 4.73). Ankle-boots were usually of Scythian style, known probably as *xshumaka*, and were tied in place by leather bands which passed around the ankle and under the sole.

Sarmatians are almost always depicted bare-headed in art – oddly, in view of winter temperatures on the Eurasian steppe. Like other ancient 'barbarians' each Sarmatian group probably had its own style of headgear, but few details survive. The Scythian custom of reserving red as the colour of the military aristocracy (Yatsenko, p.758) is also seen in grave goods, where leather garments and items of military equipment are often dyed red (see Plate B).

Although the Sarmatians produced most of their own costume and weapons, luxury goods were either looted on raids or imported.

4 When discovered, the Pazyryk tombs were dated to the 5th century BC, but recent (1996–98) carbon-14 and dendrochronology studies have revised this to 350–240 BC.

Herodotus (4.24) in the 5th century BC referred to a trade route from the Black Sea centre of Olbia, at the mouth of the Bug and Dnieper rivers, which penetrated eastwards deep into Sauromatae territory. The frequent appearance in burials of Chinese Han dynasty bronze mirrors indicates that goods – including silks – were filtering through from the Far East. The Greek centres on the Black Sea had for centuries produced goods for the Scythian market. With the arrival of the Sarmatians much of this trade switched to the Bosporan capital Panticapaeum (modern Kerch) and to Tanais at the mouth of the Don. This was a Greek 'emporium', where nomad goods and slaves were bartered for all the refinements of the Greek world, including finished clothing (Strabo 11.2.3, 7.4.5).

The Aorsi, and later the Alans, controlled the main camel routes from the Black Sea to Mesopotamia and India, bringing them great riches, and according to Strabo (11.5.8) they 'wore gold' in their dress in consequence. Oriental objects turn up in the graves of richer individuals, often making it possible to distinguish Aorsi and Alan remains from those of other Sarmatian peoples.

# ORGANISATION & TACTICS

According to the Classical writers, Sarmatian armies ranged in size from thousands to hundreds of thousands, but it is unlikely that these figures are accurate. Throughout history nomad cultures have habitually exaggerated their strength to inspire fear. Archaeological finds suggest that such huge numbers could only have been fielded by turning out all men capable of bearing arms.

Each Sarmatian people had its own 'king', who led the armed forces of his nation or Sarmatian contingents in Roman, Bosporan, Gothic and Hunnic armies. It would seem that each Sarmatian people had only one king, but literary references are too few to establish even rudimentary king lists. The royal names are usually Iranian in form, such as Aripharnes, king of the Siraces (c.310 BC), Rasparagnus, king of the Roxolani (c.AD 180), and Sangiban, king of a branch of the Alans (c.AD 450). During the disturbances on the Danube in the 350s AD the 'Free Sarmatians' had a number of tribal chiefs or sub-kings: Rumo, Zinafer and Fragiledus, who accompanied a prince and later Roman client-king, Zizais (Amm. 17.12.11).

Aristocrats such as these commanded their own troops, presumably raised from among their dependents, as Tacitus (*Hist.* 3.5) says of the Iazyges. Each such group of followers may have taken the field as a separate tactical unit. In early times every male able to bear arms served as a warrior when required. From the 4th century BC there is archaeological evidence for a 'warrior caste' in some Sarmatian tribes, centred on tribal leaders and aristocrats. The sinews of this warrior society were the personal bond and oaths of friendship and loyalty, sworn on the sword and sealed by drinking drops of each other's blood mixed with wine.

One of the 'Kosika vessels' showing Sarmatian warriors of the 1st or 2nd century AD. The origin of these vessels, found in a Sarmatian cemetery at Kosika, 110km north of Astrakhan, remains controversial. The upper register of the 21cm-high silver vessel shows a hunting scene with an unarmoured rider skewering a wild animal with his lance. A mounted archer with a small composite bow, and a wounded riderless horse, appear in the lower register. (After M.Yu.Treister, in *Vestnik Drevnei Istorii*, 1994, 1)

An interesting insight into how Sarmatian forces were raised is given by the 2nd century AD Greek author Lucian. Although his description refers to a small band raised for a punitive expedition, he indicates that larger forces could be raised in the same way: 'When a man who has been wronged by another wishes to avenge himself but sees that by himself he is not strong enough, he sacrifices a bull, cuts up and cooks the meat, spreads the hide out on the ground, and sits on it, with his hands held behind his back like a man bound by the elbows … The meat of the bull is served up, and as the man's kinsmen and all else who wish approach, each takes a portion of it, and then, setting his right foot upon the hide, makes a pledge according to his ability – one that he will furnish five horsemen to serve without [expecting to be given] rations or pay, another ten, another still more, another foot-soldiers, heavy-armed or light-armed, as many as he can, and another simply himself, if he is very poor. So a very large force is sometimes raised on the hide, and such an army is especially dependable as regards holding together and very hard for the enemy to conquer…' (*Tox.* 48).

Lucian indicates that each leader brought with him a number of horsemen or foot soldiers and was expected to supply and equip them himself. He later adds that forces of many thousands could be raised in this way 'on the hide'. Such a military structure is not dissimilar from early medieval practice or, indeed, from contemporary Germanic and Celtic systems.

By contrast, most Roman writers give the impression that the Sarmatians were a disorderly rabble, out only for plunder: 'These tribes are more suited for predatory incursions than for regular warfare' (Amm. 17.12.1); 'The Sarmatians, a tribe most accomplished in brigandage' (Amm. 16.10.20). Strabo (7.4.6) is somewhat kinder when he states that the Roxolani were 'warriors rather than brigands', but often provoked war as a way of exacting tribute.

The thirst for plunder led many Sarmatians to enroll with foreign powers – in effect, as mercenaries. Sarmatian contingents are often mentioned in the employ of the Bosporan and Pontic kingdoms. Tacitus (*Ann.* 6.32–35) notes that during a succession war in Parthia in AD 34–35 the Sarmatian chiefs, 'as is the national custom, accepted gifts from and enlisted on both sides'. When it came to blows and the Sarmatians faced a richly equipped Parthian army, their employer urged them to battle by pointing out that while they faced many enemies, this only increased the potential loot.

The Roman stereotyping of Sarmatians as undisciplined raiders continues well into the 4th century AD, even though by this time they were militarily well organised and capable of tactical subtlety. In particular the rise of the armoured lancer had brought changes. The long lance or *contus* required specialised skill in both

**'Duelling scene' from another of the Kosika vessels – see Plate G. The scale-armoured rider is about to deliver the deathblow with his contus, which has a huge head. His opponent, already struck by arrows, is unarmoured except for his thick jacket, and carries only a sheathed bow. His saddle is clearly of 'horned' type, with characteristic triple straps hanging from the rear. The cheekpieces of both horsemen's bridles are of 'propeller' form, a variety common across the western steppes until the 2nd century AD. H.von Gall, *Stsena poedinka vsadnikov na serebryanoi vaze iz Kosiki* ('The horsemen's duel on a silver vessel from Kosika'), *Vestnik Drevnei Istorii*, 1997, 2, p.174–98**

men and horses, and led to a degree of 'professionalisation', especially in detachments gathered around the aristocracy. The days of the mass tribal levy were over. There is a noticeable decline in the number of Sarmatian burials with weapons from the 2nd century AD onwards, suggesting that not all men were now warriors.

## Sarmatian tactics and the armoured lancer

The archaeological evidence suggests that for most of Sarmatian history the greater part of any Sarmatian force was composed of horse-archers. However, the most important and effective component was undoubtedly the armoured lancer, and it is upon this element that Classical authors concentrate almost exclusively.

The term *cataphract* (Greek for 'covered with armour') is often used to describe this new cavalry type. Historians have developed the habit of using it for nearly all heavy cavalrymen of antiquity, but not always correctly: we do not know the term the Sarmatians themselves used. (A more appropriate term, as we shall see, might be the Greek *kontophoros*, '*contus*-bearer', or its Latin equivalent *contarius*.)

But where and when was the armoured lancer 'invented'? The most likely answer is on the plains that extend from north-eastern Iran into Transoxania and Central Asia. A heavy cavalry tradition existed in this region back to the 5th century BC and earlier, notably among the Bactrians, Chorasmians, Massagetae and other Saka nomads. The first convincing evidence for armoured lancers appears in the 2nd century BC in Parthia, both in pictures and written accounts, but lance-armed heavy horsemen had probably appeared at least a century earlier. It has been suggested that the addition of the lance to the traditional Iranian heavy armour panoply was a response to the *sarissa* pikes of Alexander the Great's infantry when he conquered Transoxania (330–327 BC). However, since the addition of the *contus* would still not allow cavalry to charge pikemen, it seems more likely that it shows the influence of the *xyston* lances of the Macedonian cavalry. It is quite likely, then, that armoured lancers were present in Transoxania by the 3rd century BC.

The first traces of the Sarmatian armoured lancer appear in the Volga region in the 3rd and 2nd centuries BC, as evidenced by finds of the lancer's weapon-set: scale armour, large spearhead and long sword. The troop-type might easily have reached this region through contacts or forgotten wars with the neighbouring Massagetae or Sakas (as we have seen, the descendants of the Massagetae would eventually become part of the Alan confederation). But the first written records of Sarmatian armoured lancers do not appear until some time later.

The earliest record of Sarmatian cavalry in action appears in Diodorus' account (20.22–26) of the battle of Thates River (310/319 BC) in the Kuban, when King Aripharnes of the Siraces came to the aid of the Bosporan pretender Eumelos. Aripharnes formed up his cavalry, probably Sarmatians (Diodorus fails to specify their nationality) in the centre of Eumelos' battle-line of 22,000 foot and 20,000 horse. Facing them was a mixed force including Greek mercenary and Scythian foot and Thracian peltasts, together with a large body of choice Scythian horse, which Diodorus states had been deployed 'according to Scythian custom' in the centre of the line. When these Scythians charged, Aripharnes' cavalry were immediately swept away, and the battle quickly ended. The

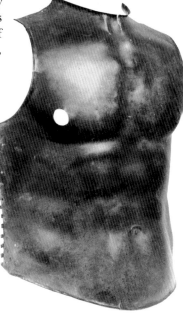

Bronze breastplate of a Greek 'muscle' cuirass, late 4th century BC, said to have been 'pulled from the Volga' on Sarmatian territory in the 19th century. Another cuirass, of iron, was found in the Volga region at Prochorovka near Orenburg, but crumbled to pieces when clumsy excavators attempted to put it on. These cuirasses may have reached Sarmatian hands via the Bosporan Kingdom or as war booty, but being uncomfortable on horseback they were probably not used very widely by the Sarmatians. (Polish Army Museum, Warsaw)

RIGHT **Suit of scale armour on the pedestal of Trajan's Column. The belt also appears to be made of scales sewn onto a leather backing. There is no obvious method for unfastening the corselet garment.**

A mysterious banded armour corselet, possibly Sarmatian, from the pedestal of Trajan's Column. It seems to be made of thick leather bands butted together on a textile or leather backing which continues as a skirt. The banded section would entirely cover the wearer's hips. The row of buckles down the front are not dissimilar to those used on the upper plates of a Roman *lorica segmentata*.

deployment of the Sarmatian cavalry in the centre of the line argues against them being purely horse-archers; but since they were unable to withstand the Scythian horse, it is unlikely that they were lancers.

Over the following two or three centuries the Sarmatians were able to overrun the Scythian territories north of the Black Sea. It is often said that it was the Sarmatian armoured lancer that gave them the edge over the Scythians, but written records are sparse, and it is unclear whether success was due to superior military technology or to other factors. If anything, the texts suggest that the Sarmatians who moved into the Pontic steppe did not yet have the armoured lancer. Strabo's brief account (7.3.17) of the Chersonesos war of 107 BC suggests that the Roxolani, who were already well established near the Crimea, had not yet adopted the *contus*. In this war the Pontic king's general Diophantes, with just 6,000 troops, was able to defeat and destroy a combined force of 50,000 Roxolani and Scythians. Strabo describes the equipment of the Roxolani: 'They use helmets and corselets made of raw ox-hides, carry wicker shields, and have for weapons spears [Greek: *longchas*], bow and sword'. He adds that most other barbarians (i.e. nomads) were also armed in this way; and comments, 'all barbarian races and light-armed peoples are weak when matched against a well-ordered and well-armed phalanx'.

The Aorsian cavalry who served in the Bosporan War of AD 49 appear to have fought in a light-cavalry role. The Aorsi were instructed to fight the army's cavalry actions, allowing the Roman and Bosporan infantry to concentrate on siege operations. On the march the Aorsi led the van and brought up the rear (Tacitus, *Ann.* 12.15). This does not mean that the Aorsi had no lance-armed troops, but lancers are yet not visible in the sources.

Only in the 1st century AD do clear written descriptions of lance-armed Sarmatian cavalry appear. The first is Tacitus' account (*Ann.* 6.33–5) of a battle fought in AD 35 in Armenia by Sarmatian mercenaries hired by King Pharamenes of Iberia in his war against the Parthians. The battle began when the Parthian horse-archers, who were 'expert at withdrawals as well as pursuits', opened ranks to allow themselves room to shoot: 'But the Sarmatian horsemen on the other side, instead of shooting back – their bows being inferior in range – charged with lance [*contus*] and sword. At one moment it was like an orthodox cavalry battle, with successive advances and retreats. Next the riders, interlocked, shoved and hewed at one another.' With the dangerous enemy cavalry force engaged by the Sarmatians, Pharasmenes then charged his fierce mountain infantry into the cavalry mêlée, and so decided the battle. Here, then, was the Sarmatian shock attack with the *contus* – not of a single disorderly mass of cavalry, but apparently of several squadrons, manoeuvring with skill and continuing at close quarters with the sword.

The next description of Sarmatian lancers comes during a raid on Roman Moesia in the early spring of AD 69. On this occasion, 9,000 Roxolanian horsemen were caught during the spring thaw by a Roman legion with auxiliaries. Overburdened with booty and slipping in the soft snow and mud, they were unable to put up much of stand, and the greater part were massacred. Tacitus (*Hist.* 1.79) notes that the weight of the armour worn by the Sarmatian 'leaders and most distinguished persons' meant that riders who were toppled from their mounts 'had difficulty regaining their feet'. Similarly, 'they could make no use of their lances or their swords [*gladii*], which being of an excessive length [*praelongos*] they wield with both hands'. (Modern commentators suggest that Tacitus was careless in his wording and that the two-handed weapon of excessive length refers to the lance rather than the sword. This may well be so, and *gladius* suggests a short sword – though P.Cornelius Tacitus was the most meticulous of Latin stylists.)

Tacitus admitted the exceptional nature of this Sarmatian defeat, for in normal conditions 'when they charge in squadrons [*turmae*], hardly any battle-line [*acies*] can stand against them'. In summary, then, Tacitus describes the complete Sarmatian lancer panoply of scale armour, *contus* and sword, employed by horsemen who charge in ordered squadrons.

The next useful description comes later in the 1st century AD from the poetic pen of Valerius Flaccus in his *Argonautica* (6, 233+): 'A fierce band of Sarmatians came thronging with savage yells; stiff are their corselets [*lorica*] with pliant mail [*molli catena* – 'supple chains'], and such too the armour [*tegimen* – 'covering'] of their steeds; but, stretching out over the horse's head and shoulders the fir-wood shaft [i.e. lance], firmly resting on their knees, casts a long shadow upon the enemy's field, and forces its way with all the might of both warrior and steed.'

Particularly interesting are Flaccus' references to armoured horses, and the great length of the lance. He continues by describing how the lumbering Sarmatians were outwheeled by their lighter opponents. It should be said that Flaccus was not a military man, and it is unlikely that he ever saw Sarmatians in the flesh. For what it is worth, his mention of 'savage yells' is corroborated by other authors who comment that the Sarmatians and Alans howled loudly as they attacked.

Several snippets of information survive concerning the Alan raid into Parthian territory in AD 135. In his 'Battle order against the Alans' the Roman provincial governor Arrian describes the Roman battle formation he ordered to be used against them. From the text it is clear that Arrian expected the Alan cavalry to launch a frontal charge, which he hoped to halt by arming his legionaries with long spears. He also expected an outflanking attack and feigned retreat aimed at disordering his formation, and gave orders to counter these threats. In his 'Tactical Manual' (*Ars Tactica*) written perhaps in AD 137, Arrian makes clear that the Sarmatian and Alan cavalry were armed with lances – and he calls them *kontophoroi*, '*contus*-bearers' rather than cataphracts. He also comments about their armour in the final (damaged) line of his 'Battle order': 'The Scythians [an anachronism for Alans], being lightly armed and having unprotected horses…'.

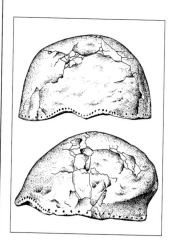

Reworked Greek bronze helmet of the late 5th century BC, found in a Sauromatian barrow near the village of Nikol'skoe on the lower Volga. The skull has been cut down in Scythian style, so that only the top 14cm remains. The helmet was found with a number of scales, probably from a neckguard that was fitted to the holes along the helmet's lower edge. (After I.P.Zasetskaya, in *Skify i Sarmaty* – 'Scythians and Sarmatians', Kiev, 1977)

A characteristic 'barbarian manoeuvre' of the Sarmatians noted by Arrian (*Tact.* 44) was the feigned retreat: 'The turns and feigned retreats of the Sarmatian and Celtic lancers', says Arrian, as well as making an impressive sports display, could be 'useful in battle'. Whether feigned retreats were adopted by the Roman horse is unknown, but the *kontophoros*, known by the Latin term *contarius*, entered Roman employment at about this time.

The standard Sarmatian offensive repertoire was repeated by the Iazyges during the battle against Romans on the frozen Danube in AD 173, a battlefield chosen, says Dio Cassius (72.7), since Sarmatian horses were able to move on ice. Part of the Iazyges force engaged the Romans frontally, while another part made a wide arc and attempted to attack from the rear. Roman discipline combined with clever use of shields to grip the ice foiled the attack, which was defeated with heavy loss.

Intriguingly, Cassius writes that Sarmatian horsemen who fell from their mounts were easily defeated by Romans on foot, since their light armour gave inadequate protection. This, and Arrian's comment about the lightness of Alan armour, have led to a theory that the powerful Hunnish bow, which first appeared at about this time, negated the battlefield value of heavy armour. In the 4th century Ammianus (31.2.21) wrote that the Alans owed their mobility to the lightness of their armour, whereas elsewhere (17.22.2) he states that the Sarmatians wore armour made from horn scales. Some historians interpret this to mean that most Alans wore no armour, as seems to have been true of the Huns. Another suggestion is that this 'lightened' armour was in fact mail, which was gaining popularity across Europe and Asia at this time.

It is surprising that a recent survey of archaeological finds (Simonenko 2001, p.305) suggests that the Alans were more heavily armoured than most Sarmatian groups except the Siraces. All along the Sarmatian cavalry had never been particularly well armoured: they were not, by definition, *catafracti*, 'covered with armour'. We have seen that Tacitus stated that it was only the 'leaders and most distinguished persons' who wore armour. The expense of such armour clearly restricted it to a social elite – a small but important and highly visible part of any Sarmatian force. The bulk of Sarmatian lancers probably never wore much armour, even before the appearance of the Hunnish bow.

There is evidence, however, that as the Roman empire collapsed and more troops took to fighting mounted, Alan armour got heavier. The Goth historian Jordanes (*Get.* 261), writing of the battle on the Nedao River in Pannonia in AD 453, characterises the Alan contingent as 'heavy-armed'. Writing somewhat earlier, in the 390s, Vegetius (*Epitoma*, I.20) complained that while late Roman infantry were now going unarmoured (a statement questioned by modern historians), the Huns, Goths and Alans 'had contributed to progress in Roman cavalry arms.' In summary, however, it was never particularly the weight of Sarmatian and Alan cavalry armour that impressed the Romans, but rather the speed and force of their attacks. Vegetius (III.26) singled out above all the superb horsemanship of the Alans and Huns – whom he considered one nation – as an ideal to be imitated by the Romans.

## Infantry and slaves

Most Sarmatian actions described by ancient authors seem to have been

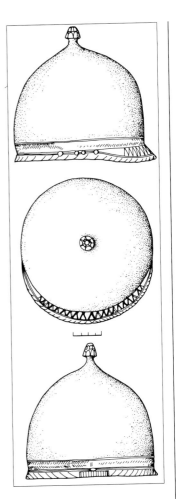

Side, top and front views of a bronze helmet of Celtic 'jockey-cap' type, found in a Sarmatian barrow near Sergievskaya, Krasnodar region, Russia; it is 20.2cm tall, with an internal diameter of 20cm. The 'peak' is actually a neckguard; and four holes at each side of the rim indicate that cheekpieces were once attached. Helmets of this type are found from the lower Danube to the Volga – evidence of extensive Sarmatian contacts with the Celts and Galatians.

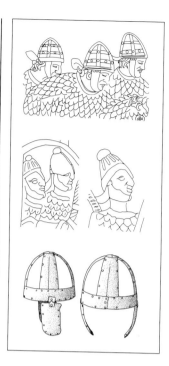

Early *spangenhelm* helmets:
TOP **Roxolani lancers from Trajan's Column**
CENTRE **Sarmatian? guardsmen from the Arch of Galerius**
BOTTOM **Helmet found in Egypt, now in the Rijksmuseum, Leiden (the neckguard is missing).**

fought with cavalry alone. Indeed, the Alans regarded it 'beneath their dignity to go on foot' (Amm. 31.2.20). The Sarmatians did, however, employ foot troops. In a semi-historical text Lucian (*Tox.* 39) indicates that 10,000 horse and three times as many foot took part in a Sarmatian raid over the Don into Scythian territory. Although Lucian wrote in the 2nd century AD, this raid is evidently set several centuries earlier. These foot troops were probably dependent peoples rather than full-blooded Sarmatians. We have seen that Lucian described warriors raising troops 'on the hide' as contributing cavalry or 'foot soldiers, heavy-armed or light-armed', depending on their means.

The Sarmatians, like all steppe nomads, maintained a parasitic relationship with their subject populations. The indigenous tribes of the Black Sea coast – often called *georgi* ('farmers') or 'agricultural Scythians' – were allowed to tend their lands in return for regular tribute. Among them were Maeots and the neighbouring Sindi, 'driven by whips' (Val. Flacc., *Argo.* 6). In AD 49 the Siraces offered to hand over to the Romans 10,000 'slaves', probably native serfs, in return for sparing the town of Uspe (Tacitus, *Ann.* 12.17).

These subject nations were often sufficiently organised to raise troops, build fortifications and revolt against the nomads (Strabo 7.4.6). Many such revolts must have occurred, though few were recorded. In the 330s AD the slaves of the Danubian Sarmatians revolted; after renaming themselves as the 'Limigantes' they followed an independent existence until 359, when, after treacherously attacking the emperor Constantius for a second time, they were massacred by the Romans. Limigantes forces were made up of infantry who advanced in close order, but also included 'nimble squadrons of cavalry' (Amm. 17.13.9).

# ARMOUR & SHIELDS

Sarmatian weaponry was influenced by their neighbours, from Central Asians to Persians and Celts. The Scythians and Thracians both employed armoured cavalry and doubtless played a role in the evolution of the Sarmatian mounted arm. Contacts with the Bosporans must also have been two-way, with Greek and eventually Roman influences percolating into Sarmatian weaponry. Less well known is the influence of the Sarmatians' long-term neighbours, the Maeots (from the shores of the Sea of Azov) and other nations of the northern Caucasus; these were militarily advanced, but bulk less large in the popular imagination.

The ancients, however, saw the greatest similarities with the Parthians. Pomponius Mela (3.3) wrote that the Sarmatians 'in both habits and arms are closest to the Parthians'. Direct contacts with the Parthians were not lacking, but this influence was largely the result of a shared Iranian-nomad origin and the links both peoples maintained with Central Asia.

### Body armour

In the early period the Sarmatians' most popular form of armour seems to have been made of leather. Strabo (7.3.17) writes that the Roxolani in c.107 BC were equipped with 'helmets and corselets made of raw ox-hides'. Speaking of the Roxolani in AD 69, Tacitus (*Hist.* 1.79) mentions that their armour was 'made of iron plates [*ferreis lamminis*] or very tough hides [*praeduro corio*]'. Some historians have attempted to identify this leather armour with a mysterious suit shown on the pedestal of Trajan's Column, made apparently of leather bands (see page 17, top). Another possible interpretation is hardened leather armour of the type used for Greek cuirasses. It is more likely that the leather armour was either a thickened variety of standard nomad leather clothing, or scale armour made from hardened leather scales.

Certainly, the characteristic armour garment of Sarmatian cavalry was the scale cuirass. Archaeological finds suggest that by the 6th century BC higher-ranking Sauromatian warriors were already wearing cuirasses covered with iron and bronze scales, much like their Scythian neighbours. Less wealthy warriors appear to have sewn individual metal plates to their leather nomad garments, especially on the upper chest.

There are no pictures that can be identified with confidence as representing Sarmatians wearing scale armour until the 1st century AD. These images show a short-sleeved garment reaching usually to the mid-thigh, with a slit at each side extending up to the belt to facilitate riding. The neck and edges of sleeves and skirt are often shown in red-brown or mid-brown colour, representing the leather base of the corselet or an arming garment. A leather belt secures the cuirass high around the waist, taking much of its weight off the shoulders. Nowhere do we see how the suit unfastened in order to be put on.

The remains of over 60 metal scale corselets have been excavated, but they have so far defied convincing reconstruction. Excavated scales are usually of iron, more rarely of bronze. They vary greatly in size from 2cm x 1.5cm to 6–8cm x 2cm and are usually rectangular, with rounded lower corners. There are varying numbers of holes bored through the top edge, allowing the scale to be threaded with copper or iron wire or leather thongs to a leather or linen base. Scales were laid much like roof tiles, in horizontal rows, with each successive row partly covering the layer below. Bronze and iron scales in alternate rows were found in the 4th or early 3rd century BC Hutor Kashcheevka *kurgan* (burial mound). By the 3rd century AD a few larger rectangular plates appear, hinting at the use among the Alans of some Asiatic laminar armour.

The earliest Sarmatian mail armour comes from the Kuban and has been dated to the 1st century BC (the neighbouring Maeots had used mail a century or two earlier). A Celtic or Galatian invention, mail armour was comfortable to wear and provided good ventilation, although it offered inferior protection against close-range archery. The Sarmatians first wore mail in mixed suits, the torso being covered by the less technologically demanding scale, while the limbs and skirt were of mail. Complete mail corselets began to replace scale armour by the 2nd century AD.

It is also from about the 2nd century AD that the first references appear to a 'low-tech' variant of Sarmatian scale armour made from horse-hooves or horn. This is mentioned for the first time by the travel writer Pausanias (1.21.8), who states that such materials were employed because of the Sarmatians' lack of access to iron. Pausanias goes on to describe a Sarmatian cuirass made of horse hooves, then preserved at the temple of Aesculapius in Athens:

'They collect hooves and clean them out and split them down to make them like snake-scales – you will not go far wrong if you think of this hoof-work like the notches of a pine-cone. They bore holes in these

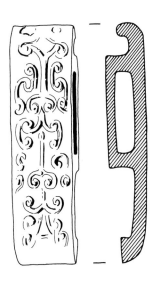

The scabbard-slide was a popular method for slinging the sword in Central Asia, Iran and northern India, and spread to Sarmatian territories by the end of the 1st century AD. Though later made of metal, the finest examples of Chinese manufacture used stones such as jadeite and chalcedony; this one, found at an unknown site in the Kuban, is made from green nephrite (kidney stone) covered in Chinese-style scrollwork, and measures 9 x 1 x 0.6cm. The slide was secured to the scabbard slightly above its centre of gravity, and allowed the scabbard to slide freely on a subsidiary belt attached below the waist belt.

scales and sew them with horse- and cattle-hair to make breastplates no less good-looking than Greek ones, and no weaker; they stand up to striking and shooting from close range.'

Similar scale armour made of horn is mentioned by Ammianus (17.12.2) worn by Sarmatians who were raiding Pannonia and Moesia in AD 358: 'These people, better fitted for brigandage than for open warfare, have very long spears [*hastae*] and cuirasses made from smooth, polished pieces of horn, fastened like scales to linen shirts.' Virtually no trace of armour made from scales of horn, hoof or hardened leather has so far been found in Sarmatian burials.

## Helmets

Finds of metal helmets, like body armour, are relatively rare and usually belonged to noblemen. The earliest Sarmatian helmets are similar to those employed by the Scythians. The Sarmatians, like the Scythians, imported helmets from the Greek Black Sea colonies. Corinthian helmets were especially popular, as seen on the famous Solokha gold comb (see MAA 137, *The Scythians*, p.14–15). Such helmets restricted vision, so the Scythians often cut away the lower parts. A reworked Corinthian helmet was found in a late 5th century BC Sauromatian *kurgan* near the Volga – no doubt an import via Scythian territory.

Besides such early headgear, barely 40 helmets (whole or fragmentary) of 2nd century BC – 4th century AD date have been found in Sarmatian sites north of the Black Sea. Most of them are of Greek *pilos*, Celtic and Etrusco-Italic varieties. The Celtic helmets are mainly of 'jockey-cap' style (H.Russell Robinson's Montefortino A/B type). Crude workmanship suggests that many were made locally. The remaining Celtic and Etrusco-Italic helmets may be imports from the neighbouring Celto-Germanic Bastarnae tribe; or are linked with the Galatians (Celts from Asia Minor) who, as recent discoveries show, maintained close relations with the Sarmatians and Bosporans.

Towards the end of the 1st century BC a new type of helmet gained popularity. It was made of curved iron plates attached beneath an iron skeleton of three or four vertical bands (German, *Spangen*) riveted to one or two horizontal hoops. Helmets of this type are worn on Trajan's Column and on Bosporan funerary reliefs and tomb paintings, but nothing similar has so far been excavated. Some of the Bosporan images show a helmet of 'Parthian' shape – rounded when seen from the side, but narrow from the front (see MAA 175, *Rome's Enemies (3): Parthians and Sassanid Persians*). Most surviving Parthian helmets are,

however, of later date. This Sarmatian 'skeleton' helmet is often said to have been the prototype for the *spangenhelm* widely adopted across Europe during the Migration period, especially among the Germanic peoples. *Spangenhelme* of an early form with a short nasal are shown worn by the emperor's bodyguard on the Arch of Galerius of c.AD 300 – a guard which is believed to have been made up of Sarmatians. But it is far from proven that these guardsmen are indeed Sarmatians, and until this key piece of evidence is better attested or further finds are made, the idea that the Sarmatians invented the *spangenhelm* must remain in question.

### Shields

Ancient shields were generally made of perishable materials such as wood, reed and leather, so little trace of them survives. One of the only Sarmatian shields so far excavated is an example from the Hutor Kascheevka *kurgan* (4th–early 3rd cent. BC) faced with metal scales, similar to Scythian shields shown, for example, on the Solokha comb. The long iron scales were joined with iron rivets, while a few rounded scales, probably from edges, had traces of a leather lining.

Otherwise evidence for Sarmatian shields is mainly literary. Strabo (7.3.17) mentions that the Roxolani horsemen of 107 BC were *gerrophoroi*, 'carriers of wicker shields'. Their shields may have resembled the leather-faced examples shown in Scythian art; more likely they resembled the *gerrhon* of the Achaemenid Persians. These have been found in the Pazyryk tombs, and were made of whittled sticks thrust through an ornate leather framework, 28cm x 36cm; since they were found attached to saddles, they were clearly cavalry shields.

In a passage about Sarmatian lancers, Tacitus (*Hist.* 1.79) states that it was not the Sarmatian custom to use shields; it would seem they were kept busy enough handling their lances.

The following two excerpts, at first glance, contradict this information. In a much mis-translated passage from Arrian's 'Battle order against the Alani' (17), he states that the second to fourth ranks of his eight-deep Roman legionary formations were to throw their javelins (evidently *pila*) to transfix the corselets and shields of the charging Alan cavalry. If it did not kill them, says Arrian, the javelins' soft metal shanks would bend, rendering the horseman useless. This may, of course, be simply a formulaic description of the effect of the *pilum*. A second reference to Sarmatian shields occurs in Dio Cassius' account of the 'battle on the frozen Danube' in AD 173, where the Romans attempted to dismount their Iazyges opponents by pulling at 'their reins and shields'. Neither reference gives details of these shields; but they do suggest that at least part of the Sarmatian cavalry – perhaps the light cavalry – was equipped with them.

# WEAPONS

### Spears and lances – the *contus sarmaticus*

The terminology of spears, javelins and lances is rarely applied consistently by Roman and Greek writers, who were trained to avoid repeating words. Modern translators often cloud the issue further. Even so, the Sarmatian lance (Latin *contus*, Greek *kontos*) was such an exceptionally long weapon that it stands out above the confusion. The word had been used in Homer

OPPOSITE **Helmets from the pedestal of Trajan's Column, often considered as Sarmatian by comparison with the Roxolani figures in two scenes of the Column's main sequence, although nothing similar has been excavated or is depicted elsewhere. As with Sarmatian helmets they are built around an external framework of vertical and horizontal bands; but here the skull plates are decorated with scrollwork, diamond and wing motifs, and the helmets are surmounted by prominent spikes. The neck-guards are made of scales fixed to a leather backing (top example), and of mail (lower example). Both sculptures are damaged at the brow, and originally had cheekpieces – the inside of one seems to be visible at low left of the lower helmet.**

in combination with a bow and wicker shield. This Greek term, pronounced 'long-kha' and originally meaning barb or point, is a generic term for a spear or javelin. Ovid (writing AD 8–18) uses the Latin *hasta* for the weapon of the Iazyges (*Ibis*, 135), again suggesting a spear rather than a lance. From the 1st century AD onwards, authors like Tacitus (*Hist.* 1.79), Arrian (*Ars Tact.* 44.1) and Ammianus (17.12.2) speak of the Sarmatian and Alan weapon as the *contus*, and call its user a *kontophoros* or '*contus*-bearer'.

Spearheads are found in graves from the earliest Sauromatian period, but it is impossible to distinguish them from lanceheads since the wooden shafts have long since decayed away and there are usually no butts. Plutarch (*Crass.* 27.2) mentions Parthian cavalry lances 'heavy with iron', and so it has been supposed that lanceheads were particularly large. In reality very large heads are rarely found. Archaeologists have in the past used accompanying armour finds to decide if a head belongs to a *contus* or a spear, but since Sarmatian graves are usually too small to accommodate the full-length shaft this is somewhat suspect. One of the few examples where a length for an excavated lance has been published was a Sauromatian grave at Oktyabrskaya on the lower Don, containing a lance allegedly 3.4m long (Maenchen-Helfen, 1973, p.238). In fact the excavators merely repeated the 'well-established fact' that Sarmatian lances were of about this length, and made no such measurement themselves.

For evidence of the length of the *contus* we must turn to pictorial sources. Bosporan wall-paintings of the 2nd century AD all show a shaft of at least 3m in length, and sometimes as much as 4.5m (9ft 9ins to 14ft 9 inches). The pictorial sources show that the *contus* was not couched underarm like the medieval lance, but rather was held two-handed – the left arm aiming and supporting the weapon's weight while the right arm thrusts from the hip. This two-handed method is required by the weapon's length.

(*Od.* 9.287) for a long pole used by Greek sailors for punting. Much later the Romans applied it to the huge Sarmatian lance or *contus sarmaticus* (W.Smith, *A Dictionary of Greek and Roman Antiquities,* 1875, p.357). It even appears in Roman poetry in non-Sarmatian contexts (Statius, *Achilleid* 2.132–4; Silus Italicus, *Punica* 15.684–5).

Before the appearance of the *contus* the Sarmatians used shorter spears. Referring to the Roxolani in 107 BC, Strabo (7.3.17) describes their main weapon as a *longche*, used

The enormous length of the Sarmatian lance is perhaps exaggerated in this 19th-century copy of a 2nd-century AD tomb painting from Kerch. However, In his experiments reconstructing Roman horsemanship, Marcus Junkelmann (*Die Reiter Roms*, III, p.145+) demonstrated that lances of up to 4.5m length were still manageable on horse-back. The lancer's armour appears to be of mail but could be scale, and is worn over tightly fitting trousers and shirt. No helmets have so far been found that match this severe conical shape. The horse's mane is 'crenellated' in steppe nomad fashion. In such wall-paintings the *contus* is never seen in combination with a shield, though sometimes with a bow. One Bosporan wall painting shows a brown loop hanging from a *contus*. This might be a leather wrist strap, which also served as a means of slinging the clumsy lance over one shoulder in later Cossack fashion. However, the poet Valerius Flaccus (6.164–5) mentions 'the Sarmatian who puts a rein upon his huge lance [*ingentis frenator Sarmata conti*]'. This probably refers to the characteristic manner in which the rider held both reins and lance in his left hand. (After Rostovtsev)

**4**

(continued on page 33)

AN 'AMAZON' GETS HER MAN: THE DON FRONTIER, 5th–4th CENTURIES BC
1: Scythian light horseman, 4th C BC
2: Early Sarmatian warrior, 4th C BC
3: Sarmatian female warrior, 5th C BC

A

THE DIVINE SWORD:
PONTIC STEPPE,
LATE 1st CENTURY BC/1st CENTURY AD
1: Sarmatian heavy horseman, 1st C BC
2: Aorsian nobleman, 1st C AD

B

A SUCCESSFUL RAID: PONTIC STEPPE, 1st–2nd CENTURIES AD
1: Sarmatian noblewoman, mid-1st C AD
2: Sarmatian or Alan armoured lancer, 1st–3rd C AD
3: Geto-Dacian prisoner, c.AD 100

ON THE MOVE: LOWER DON REGION, 1st CENTURY AD
1: Alan nobleman
2: Young Sarmatian warrior

D

TRAJAN'S FIRST DACIAN WAR, AD 101–02
1: Roxolanian armoured lancer
2: Roxolanian horse-archer

1

2

GAE

E

KINGDOM OF THE CIMMERIAN BOSPORUS

1: Bosporan footsoldier, late 2nd/early 1st C BC
2: Officer of Bosporan light horse, 2nd C AD
3: Bosporan infantryman, 2nd century AD

F

DUEL ON THE STEPPE, 2nd CENTURY AD
1: Sarmatian armoured lancer
2: Sarmatian horse-archer

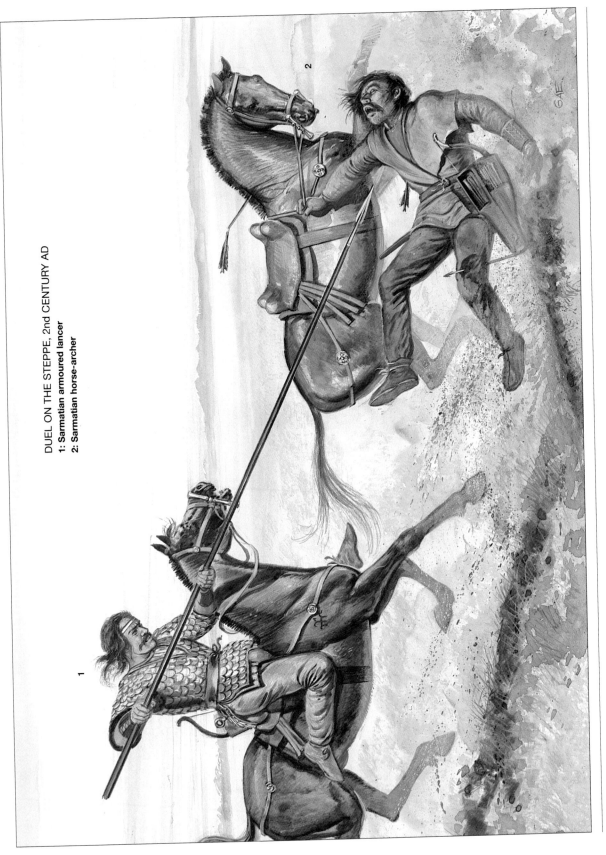

G

SARMATIANS IN ROMAN SERVICE
1: Iazygian *draconarius*, late 2nd–3rd C AD
2: Sarmatian guardsman, c.AD 300

H

## Swords

The earliest Sauromatian swords were similar to Scythian examples. Typically these were short *akinakes*, similar to those used by the Persians and other Iranian peoples, though less ornate than the examples found in Scythian noble graves.

As with the Scythians, longer Sarmatian swords begin to appear from the 6th century BC, and become common from the 4th century, though they do not displace the *akinakes*. Many of these longer swords have an antennae-shaped pommel (especially in the Volga and Kuban regions, until the 3rd century BC). From the 4th century BC the antenna pommel is replaced by one shaped like the arc of a circle (see Plate A).

The most common type of Sarmatian sword had a ring-shaped pommel as part of a one-piece iron hilt, which probably evolved by the closing of the circle on the arc-shaped and antennae-pommel swords. These began to appear in the 3rd century BC, becoming the dominant type from the 2nd century BC until the 2nd century AD. They were popular throughout the Sarmatian world, from the Danube to the Volga.

Ring-pommel swords had a short, straight metal guard and occurred in both short- and long-bladed versions. The 'short' variety was 50–60cm in length, though some were shorter. The far rarer 'long' swords measured 70cm upwards, exceptionally reaching 130cm.

Characteristic thigh scabbards for 'short' ring-pommel swords appear from the 2nd century BC. These were secured via two pairs of 'wings' by leather straps which passed around the right thigh. Sometimes the top pair of straps, or an additional pair of straps, lead to a belt hidden under the skirts of the jacket, allowing the height of the scabbard on the thigh to be adjusted. The oldest such scabbards were found in the Altai in nomad graves of the 3rd–2nd centuries BC, though these were carved wooden models, perhaps for ritual use. The 'long' ring-pommel sword was worn on the warrior's left side in a scabbard of more conventional style.

Daggers appear in Sarmatian burials throughout the period. Most had hilts of the same form as short swords of the time; indeed, the distinction is simply a matter of convention – weapons under 30–35cm (12–14ins) in length are defined as 'daggers' on that ground alone.

A unique Sarmatian adornment to ring-pommel swords was a short loop of coloured beads, typically of agate, chalcedony or glass paste. The string (usually missing in graves) was probably threaded through the ring of the pommel. Such 'sword-beads' were later used by the Huns.

The ring-pommel sword was displaced during the 2nd century AD by a new variety of long sword, which had appeared a few centuries earlier but now became the dominant type until the 5th century. These had separate pommels, typically of disc or flattened-sphere shape and made of various materials such as chalcedony or glass. Most are about 100cm (40ins) in length and had guards (quillons) of wood or bone, which rarely survive in the ground. Many such swords are found in the Volga and southern Urals regions. This type of long sword was worn on the warrior's left: excavated examples are often found in conjunction with a dagger worn on the right, attached to the waist belt. They were slung loosely by means of a 'scabbard-slide', a system of Oriental origin.

Long swords were obviously ideal for fighting from horseback. When the lance was broken or discarded (as must often have happened in the

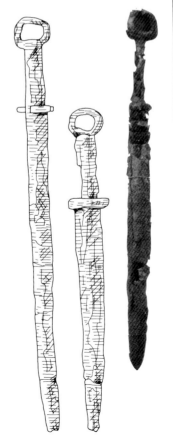

Swords with ring-shaped pommels were popular among the Sarmatians from the 2nd century BC to the 2nd century AD, and are found in great quantities in the Black Sea region and Hungarian Plain. Most were 50–60cm in length. A semi-precious stone was occasionally set in the ring of the pommel. (Archaeological Museum, Odessa)

early stages of any mêlée), the reach of the longsword allowed the continued dealing of blows from horseback. The Sarmatian horsemen who charged impetuously at the Parthians in AD 35 were equipped with sword as well as lance (Tacitus, *Ann.* 6.35), as were the Roxolani who raided Moesia in AD 69 (Tacitus, *Hist.* 1.79).

## Archery equipment

The bow was an essential part of the Sarmatian weapon-set, and though its importance declined over time it never vanished from use. The earliest Sarmatian bows were similar to Scythian examples: short, reflexed models no more than 80cm (32ins) in length and constructed of several varieties of wood glued together. From the 4th century BC bone laths were added at the grip and 'ears' (ends), giving additional power. Arrows were usually 40–50cm (16–20ins) long but could reach 60cm (24ins); they were made of birch, or sometimes of maple or poplar.

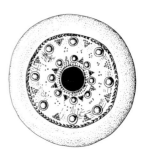

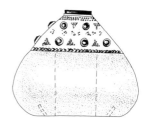

The short Scythian bow was usually kept in a *gorytos* – a combined bow-case and quiver, made mostly of leather and often strengthened and adorned with metal plaques. The *gorytos* usually hung from a belt on the rider's left hip until the long sword came into general use, after which it was often slung on the right. Separate birch-bark quivers were also employed. Excavated quivers and *gorytos* contain as many as 300 arrows, and some graves have two quivers.

Each arrow had three feather flights attached by a fine leather thong, as seen on excavated examples. Arrowshafts were often painted; some *gorytos* contained all-red arrowshafts, while a quiver found in a 4th century BC Sholokhovskii *kurgan* (Rostov-on-Don) contained 128 arrowheads with shafts painted with black, red and white bands. Presumably this 'colour-coding' indicated ownership, or allowed identification of the arrowhead type when sheathed.

During the 1st century AD a powerful new type of bow gained popularity; this is known today as the 'Hunnish' bow, though evidence of its Hun origins is inconclusive. Measuring 120cm (48ins) or more in length, it was much larger than the Scythian bow, and also of composite construction with prominent bone laths at the ears. It was usually asymmetrical in shape, with the top half above the grip being longer. Significantly more powerful than its predecessors, the Hunnish bow could draw arrows of 80cm (32ins), with heavier heads than any seen previously. Fewer arrows are found in graves of this period: most contain tens, very few have more than 100, and indeed, late Sarmatian burials seldom contain more than 15 arrows. The Hunnish bow was too large for the *gorytos*, and was instead carried in a soft bowcase alongside one or two 75–80cm tall cylindrical quivers, which were made of deerskin leather, and traditionally painted or dyed red (see illustration page 44).

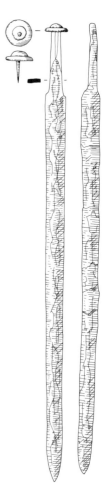

Pausanias (1.21.6) writes in the 2nd century AD of the bone points of Sarmatian weapons, in an attempt to underline the nomads' lack of access to metals. Bone arrowheads are found sporadically throughout the Sarmatian period, but not in large numbers (though bone can disintegrate when buried). In a 4th or early 3rd century BC *kurgan* near Hutor Kascheevka (Rostov-on-Don) two groups of arrowheads were found, corresponding to two quivers. In all there were 228 iron heads, four of bronze and nine of bone, the last of triangular section with polished surfaces. From the earliest times vast numbers of bronze

OPPOSITE **Late Sarmatian long swords** are typically 100cm in length and have pommels of semi-precious stone, glass or amber. Excavated examples usually lack guards (quillons), which were probably made of a perishable material such as wood or bone. The details (top) show a stone pommel with gilded metal band from a Sarmatian grave at Gradeshevka on the Lower Danube. (Archaeological Museum, Odessa, courtesy of G.Redina)

BELOW **Personal *tamga* marks** of Sarmatian rulers and Bosporan kings of Sarmatian descent:
(1) Pharzoius, late 1st century AD;
(2) Sauromates II (AD 174–210);
(3) Ininthimeus (AD 234–238);
(4) Thothorses (AD 278–308).

BOTTOM **Sarmatian horse bit**, 3rd century AD, from the Chernorechenskii cemetery, Ukraine. The mouth-piece is iron, the other components bronze. It is thought that severe bits like these were needed to control the more powerful horses of the Sarmatian heavy cavalry – although Strabo tells us that Sarmatian mounts were gelded. (After V.M.Zubar & A.V.Simonenko in *Voorozhenie Skifov i Sarmatov*, Kiev, 1984)

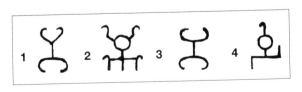

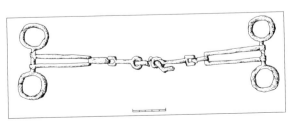

Scythian-style arrowheads turn up in Sarmatian graves. By the early Sarmatian period these have been almost entirely replaced by simple tanged heads in iron.

During his exile to the Black Sea area the poet Ovid often refers to the 'venomous arrows' of the Sarmatians: 'Among them there is not one who does not bear quiver and bow, and darts yellow with viper's bile' (*Tristia*, 5.7) – though Ovid's words may be artistic licence, reflecting his own bile at being marooned among 'barbarians'. He also mentions a collar of thorns attached round the base of the arrowhead, presumably pointing backwards to act as barbs.

### Lassos

Like most nomads in contact with cattle and wild horses, the Sarmatians employed the lasso, and Sarmatian women were said to have been especially adept in its use. Pomponius Mela (1.21.5) states that Sarmatians tossed the lasso over an enemy's neck to pull him from his horse. Pausanias (1.21.7) describes another technique: 'They throw ropes around any enemies they meet, and then wheel their horses to trip them in the tangle of rope.' The most famous use of the lasso occurred during the Alan incursion into Parthia in c.AD 73, when the Armenian king Tiridates was caught by a lasso, but managed to cut it with his sword before it tightened around his neck (Josephus, *Bell. Jud.* 7.7.4).

## HORSES & HORSE EQUIPMENT

Like all nomad breeds, Sarmatian horses were hardy animals which could survive on thin pasture inadequate for Western mounts. Their endurance was legendary. The Romans were impressed by a horse taken from the Alans during the reign of the emperor Probus (AD 276–82); though not particularly attractive or large, it was said that this mount could cover 100 miles a day, over eight to ten successive days (*Historiae Augustae*, Probus 8.3). Sarmatian raiding parties covered vast distances at speeds undreamt of by their 'civilised' adversaries, mainly thanks to the use of extra horses that were ridden in turn – one, or sometimes even two spares per rider, according to Ammianus (17.12.3).

Most Sarmatian mounts were geldings, as Strabo (7.4.8) records: 'It is a peculiarity of the whole Scythian and Sarmatian race that they castrate their horses to make them easy to manage; for although the horses are small, they are exceedingly quick and difficult to control.' One Russian study based on bone evidence from Scythian burials (quoted by M.Jankovich, *They Rode into Europe*, 1971, p.94) indicates that most horses were small Asiatic types, 13 to 14 hands to the withers (shoulder). But the Scythians also used a 'quality' breed averaging 15 hands (150cm) and similar to the modern Russian Akhal Teke – though this was confined mainly to noble burials.

Unfortunately, the Sarmatians did not have the same custom of burying horses with their owners, so there is little direct skeletal evidence. It is often assumed that Sarmatian lancers employed larger breeds and, indeed, that such mounts were a pre-requisite of the lancer's development. The Sarmatians must have had access to the most famous heavy breeds of antiquity – the Nesean, from the Nesean Plains in Media, and the related Median and Parthian breeds. Such mounts might have been acquired along the Oriental trade routes or on raids into Parthian territory. But there is little evidence for the presence of such large horses among the Sarmatians; and horses do not necessarily need to be big to be strong. Stocky build and well-formed legs are sufficient to take extra weight and, as we have seen, Sarmatian armour was not necessarily very heavy. Roman authors tend to stress the speed of Sarmatian horses rather than their size. The fully barded Roxolani mounts on Trajan's Column are not depicted as being any larger on average than the Roman cavalry ponies shown in the same scenes.

One ancient breed, the Turanian, comes close to matching the requirement of a 'quality' lancer mount, and is also a likely ancestor of the Akhal Teke. It was small and of Oriental appearance, but a true horse rather than a pony. Turanian horses originated in the Transoxania region, close to the home of the 'celestial horses' of the Ferghana valley sought after by the Chinese. Some of the superb golden bays found preserved in the ice of the Pazyryk tombs exceeded 15 hands, and were probably of a related breed. Through their contacts with the Sogdians it is entirely feasible that the Aorsi (and later the Alans) had access to these Oriental breeds.

The fast, elegant Sarmatian and Alan mounts were highly valued by the Romans. Hadrian had a favourite Alan hunter called Borysthenes (the ancient name for the Dnieper River), and an ode to this horse was inscribed on its tomb at Apt near Nîmes in France. It recounts how Hadrian rode it 'over the mounds of Tuscany… like the wind, after the boars of Hungary'.

## The 'crenellated' mane

In the Scythian period horse tails were allowed to grow freely. By the 3rd century BC, presumably under Persian influence, they were often knotted with short lengths of fabric or leather. From about the 1st century AD, judging mainly from Bosporan art, tails were allowed to grow unusually long and thin, and sometimes fitted with a braided sleeve, probably of leather. The purpose of such cuts and attachments is poorly understood, but tail-knotting was later employed by the Mongols, among whom it denoted age, sex and perhaps training status.

In the early period manes were generally hogged short, little different from Scythian or indeed Roman fashions. From about the 1st century AD (roughly when the Alans arrived near the Black Sea) the 'crenellated' mane appears. This style – resembling the battlements of a castle – had a variety of forms. Often there were just two 'crenellations', triangular rather than rectangular. These may have been purely decorative. The crenellated mane also appeared in Iran, India and China, but always as a foreign fashion imported from Central Asia. The one factor in common

Composite bow, arrow and cylindrical quiver from the pedestal of Trajan's Column. Strabo commented that the Scythian bow resembled in shape the jagged outline of the northern Black Sea coast; this bow, which is shown unstrung, is of the less extreme form which was typical of later and slightly larger Scythian bows. Note also the sword – of a non-Sarmatian type – at bottom right, the scabbard of which is slung by means of a variant of the scabbard-slide.

OPPOSITE **Detail from Bosporan funerary stele of Athenaios son of Menos, 1st century AD. The left background horseman (an ancestor?) is the only known image of a Bosporan lancer with horse armour. The bard encloses the horse's breast and appears to be of laminar construction. The rider has a conical helmet and a** contus **with a large head. Athenaios himself is unarmoured, and sits on a 'Bosporan' horned saddle. His bow is of the large Hunnish type, attached alongside two connected cylindrical quivers, cf. illustration page 44. (Kerch Museum, after Yu.M.Desyatchikov, 'Katafraktarii na nadgrobii Afeniya',** Sovetskaya Arkheologiya, **1972, 4, p.68–77)**

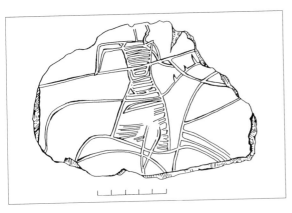

Stylised impression of an armoured lancer on a Bosporan graffito, from an early 3rd century AD Romano-Bosporan site at Iluraton near Kerch. His armour reaches down to mid-calf, longer than usually depicted in Bosporan art. The way the leg emerges from the armour suggests that the armour skirt had an opening down the side. Note the three 'spikes' of the horse's 'crenellated' mane. (After I.G.Shurgaya in *Kratkie Soobshcheniya Instituta Arkheologii,* 174, 1983)

was an Iranian-speaking people known as the Yüeh-chih or Tocharians (Maenchen-Helfen, 1957). It is likely that a section of this people joined the Alan confederacy.

### Tamga brandmarks

A characteristically Sarmatian form of brand marking is attested from about the 1st century AD – roughly simultaneous with the appearance of the Alans and of the crenellated mane. These took the form of a *tamga* – a proto-heraldic sign, akin to a property mark or monogram, which also appear on personal equipment. Several Bosporan funeral stelae show horses branded with a *tamga*, either on shoulder or haunch – see also pages 10, 35 & 46.

### Horse armour

The depiction of scale-armoured horses on Trajan's Column indicates that some, at least, of the Sarmatians' horses wore barding. The armour on the Column, which covers the horses from head to hoof, is unconvincing, and must be the result either of ignorance or of intentional stylisation. Only one other 'Sarmatian' image shows a horse bard – the Bosporan funeral stele of Athenaios (illustrated below).

Although several supposed horse armours have been found, none of the finds are reliable (Simonenko, p.298). A large expanse of mail thought to be a horse bard was found in a Sarmatian grave on the Kuban in 1896 along with two mailshirts (V.D.Blavatskii, *Ocherki voennogo dela,* 1954, p.118, no illustration). But as well as being no longer traceable, this find is difficult to date and begs more questions than it answers.

Literary references to Sarmatian horse armour are also sparse. The most detailed is by the 1st century AD poet Valerius Flaccus (*Argonautica,* 6.233–234) in his description of Sarmatian lancers quoted earlier. For lightness most horse barding was probably of leather: the Sassanian cavalry certainly used leather housings (Amm. 24.6), while the neck covering of the Dura Europos bard was made from leather scales. The use of horse armour varied between Sarmatian groups and over time.

The last (incomplete) line of Arrian's 'Battle order against the Alans' of AD 135 reads: 'The Scythians [i.e. Alans], being lightly armed and having unprotected horses...'. Yet later authors such as Contantius and Isidore of Seville seem to mention horse armour worn by the Alans (Bachrach, 1993, 'The origin of Armorican chivalry', p.167+). Clearly the Sarmatians did employ horse armour, though not on the same scale as the Parthians and Sassanians.

### Stirrups and the 'horned' saddle

It has long been assumed that stirrups were a pre-requisite of lance-armed cavalry, and that the Sarmatians used them very early. Even historians like Sulimirski (p.127) took the Sarmatian use of

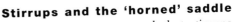

stirrups for granted. In fact, there is no good evidence for stirrups among any of the Sarmatian peoples. The earliest reliably dated stirrups are found in the 4th century AD in Korea; they reach the Central Asian steppe at the turn of the 5th–6th centuries, and arrive in Europe with the Avars in the 6th century.

The absence of stirrups does not remove the need for a stable 'seat' from which to wield the lance: the obvious place to look is the saddlery. Peter Connolly has demonstrated that the lance (and long sword) could be wielded effectively from a Roman four-horned saddle; stirrups, he discovered, were an aid to mounting, but did not give much additional stability. (They also make riding less tiring on the legs, and improve blood flow to the feet.)

Something very similar to a horned saddle appears in Sarmatian art. Bosporan tombstones of the 1st and 2nd centuries AD show a saddle with horns that partly enclose the thigh. This 'ergonomic' shape appears on more than one sculpture, so is not simply an artist's error. Sarmatian cavalry on the Kosika vessels (also 1st/2nd century AD) ride on flatter-horned saddles, more similar to the Roman version. Characteristic of these saddles were three broad leather straps hanging from the rear – probably used for securing baggage, as were similar straps in later periods.

The Parthians and Sassanians also used saddles akin to the horned type (Ghirshman, p.101–3; & Junkelmann, III, p.61); there is evidence for a saddle with a rear support divided (or 'crenellated') into two sections. It has been claimed that horned saddles were a Celtic invention, but the evidence points strongly to a Central Asian origin, with the Sarmatians as one of the main agents of transmission to Western Europe. There were, however, several varieties of horned saddle, each with its own history.

Metal discs covering junctions in the horse harness – Latin, *phalerae* – appear from the end of the 3rd century BC, and are popular in rich warrior graves during the 2nd and 1st centuries BC. They are usually of silver or silvered copper with decorated surfaces, the largest (for the breast) being 15–24cm in diameter. Smaller examples appear in pairs, and were no doubt worn on the horse's flanks.

## The draco standard

Arrian (*Ars Tact.* 35) believed the windsock-like dragon standard to be a Sarmatian invention, and such standards were being adopted by the Roman cavalry just as he was writing (c.AD 137). Their geographical origins are lost among the horse-archer societies of Central Asia, but their original purpose was probably to provide wind-direction for archery.

Arrian describes the standard as a long sleeve 'made by sewing pieces of dyed material together', which hung limp when the rider was at rest, but on the move flew like a serpent and whistled in the breeze. Arrian suggests that standards should be colourful, adding to the spectacle of cavalry parades, and that one should be given to each unit, helping maintain order, both in displays and battle.

OPPOSITE *Draconarius* (standard-bearer) on a late 2nd or 3rd century AD funeral stele from the Roman camp at Chester, England. The head of this horseman's *draco* standard is damaged and there is no inscription, but the equipment suggests that the rider is a Sarmatian. His headgear is often interpreted as a *spangenhelm*-type helmet, but might be a flower-pot-shaped felt cap. His sword appears to be fastened in Sarmatian style along the right thigh. Some authors see texturing that suggests horse armour, but this is difficult to confirm on photographs. (Grosvenor Museum, Chester, England)

BELOW *Draco* standard on the pedestal of Trajan's Column. Note the hoops to maintain the shape of the tubular fabric 'tail', with streamers attached. The staff attaches under the metal head, which resembles a dog or wolf more than a dragon. Note also the cylindrical quiver (reconstructed on Plate E); these were beginning to replace the *gorytos*.

The dragon-like gilded head of a late Roman standard was found at Niederbieber in Germany[5]. But not all such standards had dragon heads: some had just the fabric tube and no head, others had heads that resembled wolves or fishes, and Trajan's Column depicts Dacian warriors carrying standards with dog-like heads. As a group, however, such wind-sock standards are now generally termed 'draco' standards.

The dragon of the Sarmatians seems to have differed from that known to the Romans, which evolved into its present form only in the Middle Ages. The Sarmatian images were more Oriental, with more prominent ears, dog-like teeth and even fins; they did not usually have scales or the distinctive crest of the Niederbieber draco. Some Sarmatian standard heads may have represented the legendary Iranian senmurv – half-wolf, half-bird (Coulston, 1991). It is hard to say whether the dog-like draco heads on Trajan's Column reflect reality or are a Roman sculptor's interpretation of such an Oriental dragon.

Such standards were also employed by the Parthians and Sassanians; Parthian standards were said to glisten with gold and silk (Florus 1.46). In AD 357 the Roman emperors Julian and Constantius both had personal draco standards sewn from a purple material (Amm. 16.10.7; 16.12.39). Writing in the 390s AD, Vegetius (2.13) notes that the Roman infantry now also employed draco standards. They continued in use much later in the Caucasus and medieval Georgia. In Western Europe they were adopted by the Franks under Charlemagne. On the Bayeux tapestry, held by King Harold Godwinsson's standard-bearer, is perhaps the most famous of all draco standards – the Dragon of Wessex.

BELOW **Among the military gear from the pedestal of Trajan's Column is another *draco* standard, the head of a much more serpentine form than the other example illustrated; it has dagged and scalloped rings attached along the 'tail'. Beside the standard lies a mail shirt with dagged edges, secured by a narrow waist belt fastened by tying rather than buckling. The mail is worn over a pleated garment of cloth or thin leather visible at the skirt, sleeves and neck. Accompanying the suit is an elaborate *spangenhelm* which once had cheekpieces. (Author's photo)**

# LEGACIES OF THE SARMATIANS

For centuries it was believed that the Sarmatians were the ancestors of the Slavs: they lived on much the same lands; and as one people disappear in the 5th century AD, the other appears. Throughout the Middle Ages and until the 18th century the Slav world often appeared on maps as 'European Sarmatia'.

Linguists and archaeologists have long dismissed this idea; but at the same time have turned up evidence of the seminal influence of the Sarmatians on Slav language, art and religion. Indeed, it is now accepted that the Sarmatians merged in with pre-Slavic populations. Both Serb and Croat seem to be Slavicised Alan tribal names. The myth of Sarmatian origins took a strong hold in Poland, where the Alans had a minor presence. Polish heraldry has many *tamga*-like details which are often claimed to be Sarmatian. During the 17th century Polish nobles became so obsessed with the myth that they adopted nomad-influenced costume and Tatar hairstyles, and called themselves 'Sarmatians' (see illustration page 41).

5 Illustrated in Osprey Warrior series 15, *Late Roman Cavalryman 236–565 AD*, p.46

## Sarmatian influences on Roman cavalry

The Sarmatians were one of Rome's toughest and most persistent opponents. Their high-speed nomad tactics and aggressive use of mounted lancers came as an unpleasant surprise, and for a time the Romans had no means of combating them except by hiding behind the Danube. As early as AD 69 several princes of the Iazyges had been taken into Roman pay in the hope of stabilising the frontier in Moesia, though the Romans declined the services of their mounted retinues, as being too bribable to be trustworthy (Tacitus, *Hist.* 3.5). Within a few decades, however, Iazyges horsemen were fighting as allies of the Romans.

Before long the Romans began to copy the Sarmatian style of lancer cavalry, and by Hadrian's reign one of the main varieties of Roman horsemen were 'those who carry the *contus* and attack in the manner of the Alans or Sarmatians (Arrian, *Tact.* 4). Two new styles of Roman cavalry appear from this time – *cataphractii* and *contarii*. The first Roman cataphract units undoubtedly owed as much to the Parthians as to the Sarmatians, but the Roman *contarii* can be more closely tied to the Sarmatians. One of the first such units was *Ala I Ulpia contariorum miliaria*, formed very soon after Trajan's Dacian wars in Pannonia – close to the stamping ground of the Roxolani and Iazyges. A Roman tombstone of AD 145–48 from North Africa depicts a *contarius* from *Ala I Cannenefatium*, a unit which is known from inscription evidence to have drawn many of its recruits from Pannonia. This lancer is shown (in accordance with Roman sculptural convention) without armour or helmet, but wields a *contus* in the distinctive two-handed manner (Junkelmann, *Die Reiter Roms*, Von Zabern, Mainz, 1990-92, III, p.144).

As we have seen, other innovations thought to have been adopted by the Romans from the Sarmatians include the *draco* standard, and – perhaps – the *spangenhelm*. It is quite possible that the 'horned' saddle had some Sarmatian input.

The other relics of the Sarmatians are less tangible, but equally important, and some consider them to be at the very roots of Medieval chivalry.

Roman guardsmen standing either side of the emperor on the Arch of Galerius at Thessaloniki, Greece, erected before AD 311 to commemorate Galerius' war against the Persians in the 290s. Their equipment – *spangenhelm* helmets, *draco* standards and scale armour – has led historians such as Gamber to suggest that they are the Sarmatians who are mentioned fighting for Galerius by Roman authors (Orosius 7.25.12). The large round shields and *vexillum* standards indicate infantrymen, though these troops may on occasion have fought mounted. See Plate H for a reconstruction.

## The 'Arthurian connection' and the medieval knight

Of the 8,000 Iazyges horsemen exiled from their lands by Marcus Aurelius in AD 175, some 5,500

were posted to Britain, where they served in the Roman army (Dio Cass. 72.16). More than a century later a *numerus* – a term generally understood as a small unit identified by ethnicity – of about 500 Sarmatian horsemen was still stationed at Bremetennacum, modern Ribchester near Lancaster. A marble tombstone believed to identify a Sarmatian *draconarius* standard-bearer was found at Chester; and traces of the Sarmatians in Britain remain until at least AD 400 (Richmond, 'The Sarmatae, Bremetennacum veteranorum...', p.15–29).

According to some historians, the presence of Sarmatians in Britain may have given rise to the legends of King Arthur. In the time of the historical Arthur, the 5th century AD, when mounted combat was not central to the British way of war, a mounted Sarmatian contingent or their descendants who defended Britain might easily become imbued with legendary qualities. Certainly, the Sarmatian worship of a naked sword thrust into the earth has a striking echo in the Arthurian 'sword in the stone'. The great respect which swords were accorded in knightly tradition recalls practices of the Iranian nomads; while the importance of dragons in the Arthurian romances may reflect the *draco* standards. Most intriguingly, a funerary relief identifies the leader of part of the Sarmatian contingent in Britain and Gaul during the final years of the 2nd century AD as a Roman career soldier named Lucius Artorius Castus... .

It has also been claimed that the Sarmatians provided the pattern for the physical form of the Western knight. Obviously the lance was a key component of the knightly panoply; and as one wit observed, 'it is impossible to be chivalrous without a horse'. However, the essentially nomadic Sarmatian society was not remotely 'feudal'. It had the client or vassal relationship; but similar relationships existed among Celtic and Germanic societies before the arrival of the Sarmatians and other steppe nomads, and it is probably to these Germanic societies that we must look for the origins of knighthood.

After years of rubbing shoulders with the Sarmatians and Alans, the Elbe German tribes (especially the Suevi, Marcomani and Quadi), and the East German peoples (Goths and Vandals) adopted Sarmatian 'customs and arms' (Amm. 17.12.1 – referring to the Quadi). The most visible novelty was the decoration of Germanic weapons in the Scytho-Sarmatian polychrome 'animal styles' (at least four distinct types have been identified). Particularly spectacular were the jewelled sword pommels, with red garnets inset in gold – a combination which quickly spread across Dark Age Europe, notably to the Merovingian Franks.

More importantly, the Goths learned the skills of mounted combat from their nomad subjects. This 'nomadisation' of the Germanic tribes was probably the key element of the emergence of the knight in Western Europe, and was perhaps the most important legacy of the Sarmatians. The debate over the origins of chivalry remains open thanks to a theory that the Alans preserved their traditional horsemanship skills in Armorica (Loire valley area) and among the neighbouring Bretons. Bernard Bachrach has even made the intriguing suggestion that the feigned flight of the Breton contingent at Hastings in 1066 – a manoeuvre that has long confused historians – was nothing other than the characteristic nomad tactic preserved and nurtured by the descendants of the Alans.

An 18th-century Polish suit of armour made in the 'Sarmatian' style; see also R.Brzezinski, MAA 184, *Polish Armies 1569–1696 (1)*. Such armours appeared in the final years of the 17th century, a Polish flourish to the Western fad for armour *all'antica*. Jealous of Western Europeans who could claim descent from the Romans, the Poles copied what they imagined was the armour of their Sarmatian ancestors. The gorgon plaques suggest that inspiration came from armour looted from Thracian tombs rather than Sarmatian *kurgans*. (Wawel Armoury, Kraków)

# BIBLIOGRAPHY

## Primary sources

The following ancient works contain significant references to the Sarmatians. Quotations, unless indicated, are from the Loeb or Penguin editions.

Ammianus Marcellinus (AD c.330–c.395), *Rerum Gestarum* ('Histories')

Arrian (AD c.95–175) *Ars Tactica* ('Tactical Manual'); *Acies contra Alanos* ('Battle order against the Alans'). Transl. James G.DeVoto, Chicago: Ares, 1993

Dio Cassius (AD c.155–235), *Roman History* written AD c.225

*Han-Shu – Chronicle of the Earlier (or Former) Han Dynasty* (written down c.AD 90), A.F.P.Hulsewe, 'China in Central Asia – An annotated translation of Chapters 61 & 96...' (*Sinica Leidensia* XIV) 1979

Herodotus (c.485–c.425 BC), *Historiae*

Jordanes (6th century AD), *Getica* ('Origins and Deeds of the Goths'), transl. Charles C.Mierow

Josephus (AD 37–after AD 100), *Bellum Iudaicum*

Lucian (AD c.120–c.190), *Toxaris*

Ovid (43 BC–AD 18), *Tristia* ('Sorrows of an Exile'), transl. A.D.Melville, Oxford: Clarendon, 1992; pbk Oxford: OUP, 1995

Pausanias (AD c.115–after 180), *Description of Greece*

Polybius (c.200–c.118 BC), *Historiae*

Pomponius Mela (written c.43–44 AD), *De Situ Orbis* ('Geography') transl. Paul Berry, Edwin Mullen Press, 1997

Pliny the Elder (AD c.23–79), *Historia Naturalis*

Strabo (c.68 BC–c.26 AD), *Geography*

Tacitus (c.55–c.120 AD), *Annales*; *Historiae*; *Germania*

Valerius Flaccus (1st century AD), *Argonautica* ('Voyage of the Argo')

Vegetius (written c.390s AD), *Epitoma Rei Militaris* ('Epitome of Military Science'), transl. N.P.Milner, 1993

## Secondary works

The Western literature on the Sarmatians is sparse, but the following should provide a sound introduction:

Bernard S.Bachrach, *A History of the Alans in the West*, Minneapolis, 1973

Bernard S.Bachrach, *Armies and Politics in the Medieval West*, London, 1993 (collection of essays)

J.Harmatta, *Studies on the History and Language of the Sarmatians*, Szeged, 1970

V.Kouznetsov & I.Lebedynsky, *Les Alains. Cavaliers des steppes, seigneurs du Caucase*, Paris, 1997

D.Sinor (ed.), *The Cambridge History of Inner Asia*, 1990

Tadeusz Sulimirski, *The Sarmatians*, London, 1970

For more strictly **military and costume** aspects:

J.C.N.Coulston, 'The draco standard', *Journal of Roman Military Equipment Studies*, 2, 1991, p.101–14

O.Gamber, 'Dakische und sarmatische Waffen auf den Reliefs der Traianssäule', *Jahrbuch der Kunsthistorischen Sammlungen in Wien*, 60 (N.F.24), 1964, p.7–34

R.Ghirshman, 'La selle en Iran', *Iranica Antiqua*, X, 1973, p.95–107

Anne Hyland, *Training the Roman cavalry. From Arrian's Ars Tactica*, Stroud: Alan Sutton, 1993

A.M.Khazanov, *Ocherki voennogo dela Sarmatov* ('Essays on Sarmatian warfare'), Moscow, 1971 (the first systematic study of archaeological evidence)

Otto Maenchen-Helfen, *The World of the Huns*, Berkeley, 1973

Otto Maenchen-Helfen, 'Crenelated mane and scabbard slide', *Central Asiatic Journal*, 3, 1957, p.85–138

M.Mielczarek, *Cataphracti and Clibanarii. Studies on the heavy armoured cavalry of the Ancient World*, Lodz 1993. (Contains fuller bibliography of Russian and Ukrainian sources)

M.Mielczarek, *The Army of the Bosporan Kingdom*, Lodz, Poland, 1999 (available from Oxbow Books, Oxford)

I.A.Richmond, 'The Sarmatae, Bremetennacum veteranorum and the Regio bremetennacensis', *Journal of Roman Studies*, 35, 1945, p.15–29

A.V.Simonenko, 'Bewaffnung und Kriegswesen der Sarmaten und späten Skythen im nordichen Schwartzmeergebiet', *Eurasia Antiqua*, 7, Berlin, 2001, p.187–327

H.von Gall, *Stsena poedinka vsadnikov na serebryanoi vaze iz Kosiki* ('The horsemens' duel on a silver vessel from Kosika'), *Vestnik Drevnei Istorii*, 1997, 2, p.174–98

G.Widengren, 'Some remarks on riding costume and articles of dress among Iranian peoples in antiquity', *Studia Ethnographica Upsaliensia*, 11, 1956, p.228–276

S.A.Yatsenko, 'Clothing vii: of the Iranian tribes in the Pontic Steppes and in the Caucasus', *Encyclopaedia Iranica*, 5 (1992), p.758–60

For the 'Arthurian connection':

C.Scott Littleton & Linda A.Malcor, *From Scythia to Camelot: A Radical Reassessment of the Legends of King Arthur*, New York & London: Garland, 1994; revised pbk edn, 2000

# THE PLATES

Our reconstructions of Sarmatian warriors cluster around the period for which most information is available: 1st century BC to 2nd century AD. Before this period pictorial representations are scarce and warrior burials rarely contain more than a rusty sword and spearhead; after this period, Sarmatian material is scattered across Europe and intermixed with non-Sarmatian artefacts. We have resisted the temptation to show objects from too many aristocratic tombs, which might give the impression of a wealthier culture than was the case. The Sarmatians and Alans were certainly sophisticated peoples with their own traditions of craftsmanship; but the soils of southern Russia have, unfortunately, not been kind to textiles, wood and leather, and without unashamed invention we cannot hope to do justice to the rich patterns that must have appeared on clothing and horse deckings. Nevertheless, readers should bear in mind that the growing science of textile archaeology teaches us two rules of thumb: that our ancient forebears practised much more sophisticated handicrafts than was once believed, showing as much mastery of the materials and techniques of their world as we do of ours; and that the love of colourful personal display seems to have been common to most cultures and periods.

## A: AN 'AMAZON' GETS HER MAN: THE DON FRONTIER, 5th–4th CENTURIES BC

For several centuries the Don River marked the boundary between Scythian and Sarmatian territories. During the 4th century BC the Sarmatians began to infiltrate across the river, and it is from this period that Greek historians began spinning tales of Amazons, based on the fact that Sarmatian women apparently took part in warfare. Sarmatian girls were supposedly forbidden to marry until they had killed an enemy (Hippocrates, *Peri Aeron* 17) – or, perhaps more realistically, 'encountered an enemy in combat' (Pomponius Mela, 3.4).

### A1: Scythian light horseman, 4th century BC

Scythian costume is well documented thanks to the copious art created by craftsmen in the nearby Greek Black Sea colonies. This figure is taken from scenes of daily life on a gold plate from the 4th century Scythian barrow-mound of Kul-Oba in the Crimea. Textile pattern details are from mid-5th century BC woollen cloth fragments found in Kurgan 4 of the 'Seven Brothers' site. The pattern was dyed using a resist technique, while the reddish colour was painted on; the pattern on the side of the trouser legs was embroidered. He would carry a short spear and a Scythian bow, sheathed in a *gorytos* made mostly of leather. If a sword was carried it would be a simple *akinakes*, a type frequently found. For further reconstructions of Scythian warriors see E.V.Cernenko & M.V.Gorelik, MAA 137, *The Scythians 700–300 BC.*

### A2: Early Sarmatian warrior, 4th century BC

Ancient writers report that early Sarmatian costume was similar to that of the Scythians, but the archaeological record shows a somewhat poorer weapon set, with less differentiation between rich and poor burials. This figure is reconstructed from a belt-end fitting now in the Historical Museum, Moscow (illustrated on p.13). It shows a duel between two horsemen, both wearing what appear to be quilted garments which are cut like the Iranian nomad *kurta*. Weapons are a short spear and Scythian reflexed bow; and

Detail of Bosporan funeral stele of Rhodon, son of Helios, early 1st century AD. He wears a short tunic and trousers, cloak fastened on the right shoulder by a brooch, and carries a large oval shield with a small round boss. His helmet, carried by his son, has radial bands and cheek-pieces. (Hermitage Museum, St Petersburg)

'Hunnish' bow, c.1st–4th century AD, found in Central Asia at Niya in the Taklimakan Desert, Xinjiang – see Plate B. The bow, which may have reversed with age, is assymetric, of strung length 132cm; it is made of wood with bone pieces fitted at the 'ears' and grip, silk wrapping, and a string of tendon. The bowcase is of soft leather and is attached to two cylindrical deerskin quivers (one damaged) which are partly painted red. Similar bowcases are seen on Bosporan funerary reliefs. (After *Legacy of the Desert King*, China National Silk Museum, Hangzhou, 2000)

note the short antennae-pommel sword attached via a leather 'wing' of the scabbard to a scale-covered belt. As usual in Sarmatian art, this rider is bareheaded. Colourful Achaemenid Persian felt saddle cloths were highly sought after as far afield as Greece and Pazyryk in the Altai Mountains, and could easily have been acquired by Sarmatian noblemen. (Cavalry shields of Achaemenid style are also found at Pazyryk.)

### A3: Sarmatian female warrior, 5th century BC
Weapons are found in many female graves on the Volga and in the southern Urals from the 6th to 4th centuries BC, and especially during the 4th and 3rd centuries. Female graves are usually better equipped than those of men and occasionally contain small items of jewellery such as paste beads. The face is reconstructed in part from a skull of a Sarmatian 'queen' from Novocherkassk. The remainder of this costume is somewhat speculative, but is based on male costume of the time, with the addition of an arc-pommel short sword and a lasso – a known favourite weapon of 'Amazons'. Literary evidence suggests that some Sarmatians were tattooed in childhood.

### B: THE DIVINE SWORD: PONTIC STEPPE, LATE 1st CENTURY BC/1st CENTURY AD
The sword had a special place in Sarmatian religion. According to Lucian (*Toxaris*), the Scythians and Sarmatians worshipped the wind (literally 'breath') and the sword, 'one because it gave life, the other because it took it away'. Sarmatian sword ritual has recently captured the popular imagination because of similarities to the Arthurian 'sword-in-the-stone' legend. According to Ammianus (31.2.23), the Sarmatians 'plunge a naked sword into the ground with barbaric ceremonies, and then worship it with great respect as Mars, their god of war'. Horses and cattle were sacrificed on important occasions, but judging from burials, sheep sacrifice was more common. Our 'divine sword' is a typical Sarmatian ring-pommel weapon, a type which remained in use for over four centuries (2nd C BC–2nd C AD). Excavated examples sometimes have a semi-precious stone inset in the pommel. Horned saddles of the characteristic form seen in Bosporan art are shown on the horses in the background.

### B1: Sarmatian heavy horseman, 1st century BC
To judge from finds in the Kuban, combination scale-and-mail corselets appear in Sarmatian use at the turn of the 1st centuries BC and AD. The rounded iron scales are typically 2.5 x 1.5 cm, while the mail is made of 1mm-thick wire, in rings of about 9mm diameter, each attached to four neighbours. This horseman wears a new type of short sword, with a ring-shaped pommel; this is carried in a leather-faced wooden scabbard, strapped to the thigh in a manner introduced from Central Asia. The main weapon is already the long Sarmatian lance known to the Romans as the *contus*. Sarmatian spears and lances are seldom depicted with butts (metal ferrules), though several were found in a *kurgan* near Sholokhovskii village, Rostov-on-Don region; these were 25.5cm long and 3cm in diameter, and were found in association with 50cm-long socketed spearheads.

### B2: Aorsian nobleman, 1st century AD
This figure is based on a wealthy Sarmatian, probably of the Aorsi or possibly an Alan, found buried near the village of Porogi, Ukraine (reconstructed in A.V.Simonenko & B.I.Lobai, *The Sarmatians of the NW Black Sea region in the 1st C AD – Noble graves near the village of Porogi*, Kiev, 1991 – Russian text). Remains of a red leather jacket and trousers were found under the skeleton, secured by a red leather belt with gold-plated iron buckle. The jacket has sheepskin trim, and is fastened with two silvered *fibulae* brooches. The short sword lay at his right hip; it had a wooden handgrip covered with red leather, and a scabbard also covered with red leather and decorated with gold appliqué plaques, including one bearing a *tamga* property mark. Near the body were bone laths from a large composite bow of unstrung length c.120cm (47 inches). A gilt plate thought to be part of an archery armguard was also recovered. We have added a pair of cylindrical deerskin quivers and a soft leather bowcase, partly from the Bosporan funerary stele of Atta son of Tryphon, from Theodosia in the Crimea, which shows them slung on the right side of the horse behind the rider's leg; and partly from a Hunnish bow with quivers and case found at Niya in the Taklimakan Desert. These items too may have been coloured red.

### C: A SUCCESSFUL RAID: PONTIC STEPPE, 1st–2nd CENTURIES AD
Raiding in search of cattle, horses and slaves was a major occupation of Sarmatian warriors. Since the Sarmatians themselves did not generally employ slaves, these were sold in Greek market towns such as Tanais at the mouth of the Don. The nomad tent (yurt or, more correctly, *ger*) in the background is taken from a lost wall painting in the tomb of Anthesterios, at Kerch. This is one of the earliest known depictions of a nomad tent, though doubts exist about the accuracy of the 19th century copy. One modern reconstruction pictures the yurt as of rectangular form, but we follow the circular shape known from later periods.

## C1: Sarmatian noblewoman, mid-1st century AD

The burial of this 45- to 50-year-old woman found at Sokolova Mogila near Nikolaev, Ukraine, was so ornate that she is often described as a 'queen'. G.T.Kovpananeko's reconstruction has been followed here, except for minor details. Her main garments were a long purple dress and a coat, both richly decorated with gold plaques and gold embroidery. Her short leather boots were also covered with 108 gold plaques.

## C2: Sarmatian or Alan armoured lancer, 1st–3rd centuries AD

This figure, based on the Bosporan stele of Tryphon (page 9), represents the less wealthy and so more typical Sarmatian or Alan lancer at the height of their power. His armour is made from large polished horn or horse-hoof scales, sewn to a leather or linen backing, and secured by a broad leather waistbelt. No headgear of the type worn by Tryphon has been found; we restore it in hardened leather, though it might be of felt or metal. His main weapon is the *contus sarmaticus*, which the ancient authors suggest was used with a long sword. Only a few ring-pommel long swords have been excavated, and they do not appear often in art, so the method by which they were slung is not well understood. A ring-pommel short sword/long dagger might also be carried, strapped to the right thigh in the usual Sarmatian manner. According to Ammianus (31.2.22), writing of the Alans, 'The most glorious spoils they esteem are the scalps they have torn fROm the heads of those whom they have slain, which they put as trappings and ornaments on their war-horses'.

## C3: Geto-Dacian prisoner, c.AD 100

This Getic or Dacian warrior, restored from the Tropaieum Traiani monument at Adamklissi, Romania, represents a nobleman from the area immediately to the east of the steppe belt, which provided a regular target for Sarmatian raiding. Herodotus notes that the Thracians (from whom the Getae and Dacians were descended) employed cloth made from hemp, which looked like linen to the inexperienced eye. Felt caps (*pilei*) distinguished Dacian nobles (*pileati*) from the commoners (*comati*), who went bareheaded.

## D: ON THE MOVE: LOWER DON REGION, 1st CENTURY AD

In the mid-1st century AD a fresh influx of nomads arrived near the Don and to the north of the Caucasus. They had new Central Asian equipment with more powerful bows, and horses with 'crenellated' manes.

## D1: Alan nobleman

This aristocrat is reconstructed from a 1st century AD grave (E.I.Bespalyi, 'A Sarmatian kurgan near the town of Azov', *Sovetskaya Arkheologiya,* Moscow 1992, 1, p.175–191). The elegant dagger with a 23cm blade was carried in an elaborate scabbard, decorated in a manner similar to those found in the Altai. Accompanying the deceased was an ornate set of horse furniture, with cheekpieces covered in gold leaf, and gilded *phalerae* inset with semi-precious stones; we give our rider silvered fittings with blue enamel insets. The rider wears a hemp-linen shirt and loose-fitting *saravara* trousers; he has laid aside his kaftan in the heat, but a man of this wealth would presumably have fairly richly decorated clothing. Ankle shoes (*xshumaka*) appear to have been the most common type worn; surviving artefacts from the Ossetians (descendants of the Alans) are of 'turn-shoe' construction, with the soles sewn to the uppers before being reversed. The strap under the instep is to secure the shoe – it is not a stirrup-loop. Note the horse's 'crenellated' mane, and the very long tail confined in a braided sleeve. A 6th-century 'Vandal' horse depicted on a Roman mosaic from Borj Djedid, Tunisia, and now in the British Museum has on its hindquarter this *tamga* brandmark resembling a cross-fleury (see Osprey Warrior series 17, *Germanic Warrior 236–568 AD,* p.52). The Alans, of course, formed a part of Vandal strength in North Africa.

## D2: Young Sarmatian warrior

Most Sarmatian male graves of this period contain few artefacts; seldom is there more than a ring-pommel short sword or dagger and a spearhead, and on occasion a primitively made clay pot, with characteristic handle in the shape of an animal. We restore a leather *kurta* jacket worn over a hemp-linen shirt, with loose-fitting trousers and

Copy of a 2nd century AD Kerch tomb mural showing five Bosporan infantrymen. Two of them wear scale corselets painted grey to represent iron, and helmets with multiple horizontal bands, similar to those shown on Trajan's Column. The unarmoured figures wear red-brown and grey-blue tunics split at the front like the armour (cf Arrian's 'Cimmerian tunics', which were of the same shape as armour corselets). All have swords and pairs of heavy-bladed spears. (After Rostovtsev)

scale-covered belt. Some textile finds suggest bordering in e.g. 'rope twist' patterns of contrasting colours.

## E: TRAJAN'S FIRST DACIAN WAR, AD 101–02

The Roxolani played an important part in Trajan's Dacian wars, providing the Dacians with their best cavalry. They are shown only in the sections of Trajan's Column dealing with the first campaign, AD 101–02, and probably kept on the sidelines during the decisive campaign of AD 105–06. The Column is a notoriously difficult source to interpret even for the appearance of Roman troops. The sculptors may well have been ignorant of the details of Sarmatian weaponry, and perhaps deliberately stylised the Sarmatian figures to underline their non-Roman features. The war gear on the pedestal of the column is more clearly sculpted, but is difficult to attribute to the factions in the conflict. Only by comparing ancient descriptions and archaeological finds is it possible to attempt realistic reconstructions of warriors from this time.

### E1: Roxolanian armoured lancer

The stylised head-to-hoof horse armour shown on Trajan's Column must reflect some form of horse bard. Our reconstruction is based on the Dura Europos bard, together with a bard shown on the Bosporan stele of Athenaios son of Menos. A saddle of 'horned' type is probable, though none are visible on the Column. The rider's early *spangenhelm*-type helmet has been copied from the main scenes on the Column, along with its soft neckguard, apparently of leather. The armour corselet is taken from the pedestal. On the Column one Roxolanian rider has a medium-length sword slung at his right side in Roman manner: this is probably a sculptor's error. We have restored a ring-pommel short sword strapped to the right thigh in Sarmatian fashion; a long sword might also have been worn on the left.

### E2: Roxolanian horse-archer

Horse-archers are rarely mentioned by ancient authors, but probably still made up the bulk of Sarmatian strength. Sarmatian shock tactics would have worked best with horse-archers 'shooting in' the charges of the lancers, presumably using the 'Parthian shot' technique. Roxolanian horse-archers on Trajan's Column are depicted in armour similar to that of the lancers. The helmet, corselet and archery equipment are taken from the pedestal of the Column. The helmet has embossed metal decoration in Iranian style, which is mirrored in paint on the cylindrical leather quiver.

## F: KINGDOM OF THE CIMMERIAN BOSPORUS

From the 6th century BC to the 4th century AD a powerful kingdom existed in the Cimmerian Bosporus (eastern Crimea), uniting the previously independent Greek colonies. At the turn of the 1st centuries BC and AD a dynasty of Sarmatian descent seized power, and the kingdom and its fighting men were heavily 'Sarmatised'. The urban culture of the kingdom survived, and was maintained by the strong walls of the main cities – the fortifications shown here are suggested by surviving ruins and details on Bosporan coins.

### F1: Bosporan footsoldier, late 2nd/early 1st century BC

Bosporan and Sarmatian weaponry in the early period were influenced by neighbouring Celtic tribes and their Galatian cousins of Asia Minor. This footsoldier is reconstructed from a Bosporan funerary stele (V.P.Tolstikov, 'A soldier's gravestone from the Akhtanizovsky estuary', *Vestnik Drevnei Istorii*, Moscow, 1976, 1, p.80–90). His shield is a Celtic *thureos*; similar oval shields appear on Bosporan funerary reliefs and terracotta figurines from the late 3rd century BC, and are popular by the early 1st century BC. The slight thickening at the centre of the shield rib dates this figure to the late 2nd/early 1st century BC. This warrior might equally be equipped with a mailshirt, and a Celtic or Etrusco-Italic helmet.

### F2: Officer of Bosporan light horse, 2nd century AD

Unarmoured horsemen representing the urban elite are often the subject of Bosporan funerary reliefs, and our reconstruction closely follows one such stele. His equipment shows many Sarmatian influences. Foremost is the bow, which the Bosporans adopted very early from their nomad neighbours – here a compact Scythian model kept in a *gorytos*. A Sarmatian ring-pommel knife or short sword is strapped to his right thigh. Long swords, when shown, appear alongside the *gorytos* and may have been fastened directly to it. No shield is visible on this particular stela, though on some other tombstones accompanying foot figures hold oval shields which may belong to the horseman.

### F3: Bosporan infantryman, 2nd century AD

During the 1st and 2nd centuries AD the Bosporan Kingdom was a Roman dependency. We hear of 'native troops of Bosporus with Roman arms' during the Bosporan war of AD 49 (Tacitus, *Ann.* 12.15–17), and bow-armed Bosporan infantry are listed in Arrian's 'Battle-Order against the Alans' in AD 135. The appearance on Bosporan inscriptions of the rank titles *strategos, chiliarchos, lochagos* and *speirarchos* indicate that Greek military organisation persisted. This infantryman is taken from a lost wallpainting at Kerch showing five Bosporan footsoldiers. Their oval shields and pair of spears are typical of Roman auxiliary equipment. Oval shields are the main type depicted in Bosporan art; most have circular bosses, perhaps reflecting Germanic influence – this example (diameter 25cm, depth 8cm) is restored from a 2nd century AD example found at Kerch. Sarmatian influence remains strong and includes the scale armour (note the skirt split at front rather than sides), proto-*spangenhelm* type helmet, and sword worn on a scabbard slide (restored from sculptures of Sarmatian-influenced Roman troops in Hungary).

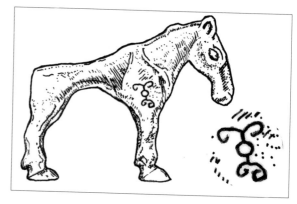

*Tamga* brand on the horse-shaped handle of a Sarmatian drinking vessel; cf Plates D and G.

## G: DUEL ON THE STEPPE, 2nd CENTURY AD

This cavalry combat follows closely a so-called 'duelling scene' on one of the Kosika vessels. The Parthian appearance of the combatants is striking – indeed, Roman authors comment that Sarmatian costume was very similar to Parthian.

### G1: Sarmatian armoured lancer

This armoured warrior carries his *contus* two-handed, steadying his aim with the left arm, while the force of the blow is provided by the right arm and the horse's momentum. His 'seat', with extended left leg, helps balance the cumbersome lance and absorb the shock of impact, greatly aided by the 'horned' saddle. The scale corselet has a V-shaped neck, exposing a separate shirt covered with smaller scales. Lancers in Bosporan tomb paintings often wear similar scale shirts under cloth or leather garments. A laced sleeve appears on the rider's right forearm on the source; this might be part of the armour corselet, but is probably an archery armguard shown on the wrong arm – ancient artists often confuse right and left. A *gorytos* is worn at the rider's left, where it will not interfere with the lance; apparently attached to it is a ring-pommel long sword. The *tamga* brand on the horse's shoulder is taken from the 1st–3rd century AD Bosporan funerary stela of Atta, from Theodosia in the Crimea.

### G2: Sarmatian horse-archer

This horse-archer appears to wear a jacket with broad 'lapels' that extend over the shoulders, apparently providing extra protection. Other figures on the Kosika vessels wear similar garments. The only weapon shown is a short reflexed bow kept in a *gorytos*, worn with an archery armguard, this time only on the left forearm. The horse furniture and saddle is revealed in detail on the Kosika vessel, and although no Eastern 'horned' saddle has been excavated, we have bitten the bullet and attempted a reconstruction.

## H: SARMATIANS IN ROMAN SERVICE

### H1: Iazygian *draconarius*, late 2nd–3rd century AD

This standard bearer is based on the Chester funerary relief. The headgear on the relief may be a felt or leather cap, but we restore a helmet based on the Leiden *spangenhelm*. The texture of the sculpting suggests a mail corselet rather than one of scale. A Sarmatian ring-pommel short sword has been restored, though only the characteristic way that it clings to the thigh

appears on the original. We have added spurs, held in place by Y-shaped bronze plates; these are of late 2nd–3rd century date, and judging from the find distribution, were popular among Sarmatians (especially Iazyges) living between the Danube and Tisza rivers in modern Hungary.

The *draco* standard is restored from the pedestal of Trajan's Column, with details added from the surviving standard head from Niederbieber, Germany. The 'tail' is made from light material, perhaps silk; extra hoops help maintain the shape and serve to attach the dagged rings of material, which fluttered in the breeze, increasing the impression, recorded by Arrian (*Ars Tact.* 35.3–4), of a flying beast.

### H2: Sarmatian guardsman, c.AD 300

This figure is taken from guards surrounding the emperor on the Arch of Galerius. Though he is clearly equipped as a footsoldier, the *draco* banners and horses on the source suggest that he might also have served on horseback. His corselet is made from scales with embossed ribs, indicating metal rather than horn – as appropriate for a guard unit. No helmet of the pattern shown on the Arch survives: it has shaped cheekpieces, a nasal and a leather neckguard – we interpret this as a proto-*spangenhelm* of Ortwin Gamber's 'late Sarmatian' type. Some guardsmen on the Arch appear to wear studded boots, a late version of *caligae* with leather uppers completely covering the foot; untypical of Sarmatian footwear, they might be Roman military issue or local replacements.

No swords are shown on the Arch, so we add a long sword with disc-shaped chalcedony pommel, slung in Central Asian manner, by means of a nephrite or jadeite scabbard-slide. The shield boss is based on an ornate example with Sarmatian ornament found at Herpaly in Hungary (Sulimirski, plate 53), and representing Goth influence on the Sarmatians during the 3rd century.

**Funerary stele of a Bosporan nobleman, 2nd century AD, partly reconstructed in Plate F. He is unarmoured, and wears a cloak and trousers; the short ring-pommel sword can clearly be seen attached in Sarmatian style to the right thigh, and a reflexed bow can be seen on the far side of the saddle. The saddle is of a Bosporan 'horned' type which partly encloses the thigh; hanging at right rear are the triple straps characteristic of horned saddles. The background horseman is a heavy cavalryman, wearing a conical helmet with cheekpieces and a corselet, probably of scale.**

# INDEX

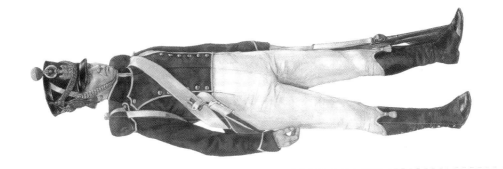

# FIND OUT MORE ABOUT OSPREY

❏ Please send me the latest listing of Osprey's publications

❏ I would like to subscribe to Osprey's e-mail newsletter

Title/rank

Name

Address

Postcode/zip             state/country

e-mail

I am interested in:

❏ Ancient world
❏ Medieval world
❏ 16th century
❏ 17th century
❏ 18th century
❏ Napoleonic
❏ 19th century

❏ American Civil War
❏ World War I
❏ World War II
❏ Modern warfare
❏ Military aviation
❏ Naval warfare

Please send to:

**USA & Canada**:
Osprey Direct USA, c/o MBI Publishing, P.O. Box 1,
729 Prospect Avenue, Osceola, WI 54020

**UK, Europe and rest of world**:
Osprey Direct UK, P.O. Box 140, Wellingborough,
Northants, NN8 2FA, United Kingdom

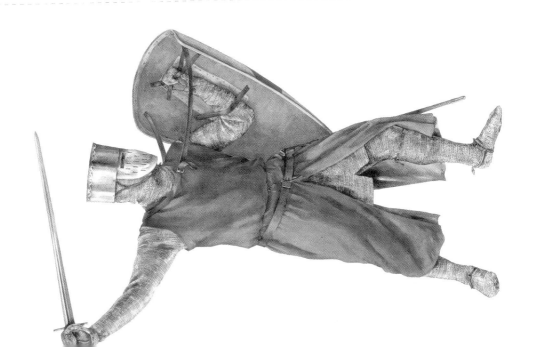

OSPREY
PUBLISHING

www.ospreypublishing.com

call our telephone hotline
for a free information pack

USA & Canada: 1-800-826-6600
UK, Europe and rest of world call:
+44 (0) 1933 443 863

**Young Guardsman**
Figure taken from *Warrior 22:*
*Imperial Guardsman 1799–1815*
Published by Osprey
Illustrated by Richard Hook

ight, c.1190
re taken from *Warrior 1: Norman Knight 950 – 1204 AD*
lished by Osprey
trated by Christa Hook

POSTCARD